FROM COMMUNISM TO CAPITALISM

A MILLIONAIRE'S JOURNEY

BENIAMIN MURESAN

Published by Self Publish -N- 30 Days

Copyright 2020 Beniamin Muresan

All rights reserved worldwide. No part of this book may be reproduced or transmitted in any form or by any means electronic or mechanical, including photocopying, recording or by any information storage and retrieval system without written permission from Beniamin Muresan.

Printed in the United States of America

ISBN: 979-8-65432-363-7

1. Non-Fiction 2. Autobiography 3. Success 4. Communism 5. Capitalism

Beniamin Muresan *From Communism to Capitalism*

Disclaimer/Warning:

This book is intended for lecture and informative purposes only. This publication is designed to provide competent and reliable information regarding the subject matter covered. The author or publisher are not engaged in rendering legal or professional advice. Laws vary from state to state and if legal, financial, or other expert assistance is needed, the services of a professional should be sought. The author and publisher disclaim any liability that is incurred from the use or application of the contents of this book.

First of all, I thank God for giving me air in my lungs and for the opportunity to live an abundant life. My faith has been the driving force behind every important decision and I would not be here without God's grace.

I dedicate this book to my parents, Vasile and Viorica Muresan, to whom I am immeasurably grateful. I want to recognize them as the most amazing humans I've ever met. These two people have sacrificed immensely and continue to pursue a life of daily, faithful purpose. I would never have recognized my purpose had they not faithfully pursued theirs. Mom and Dad, you have been amazing examples of passion, dedication, servanthood and perseverance. You have been the best role models a man could ask for and I thank you.

Mom, I inherited your passion, perseverance, empathy and your wit. It's made me the creative, compassionate and free-spirited man that I am today. Dad, I inherited your logic, focus, morality and discipline. It's these qualities that keep me grounded and calculated. Your wisdom and teachings have made a drastic impact in my life.

I truly feel blessed to have absorbed the best that two people could ever offer. I feel that it is my duty and privilege to honour your sacrifice and fulfill the journey that you started. Thanks to both of you, I can leave a real legacy, your legacy.

God bless you.

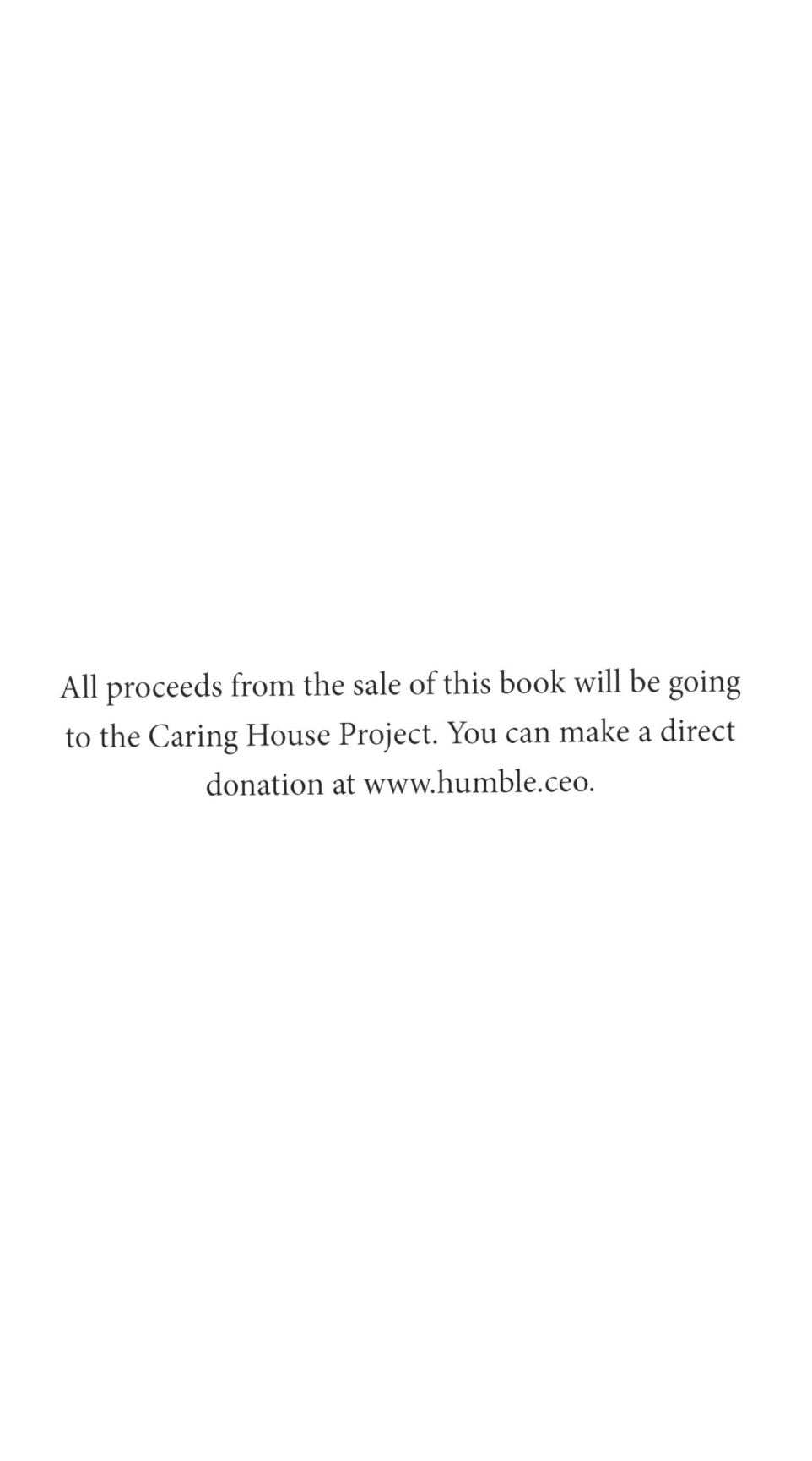

All proceeds from the sale of this book will be going to the Caring House Project. You can make a direct donation at www.humble.ceo.

CONTENTS

Acknowledgements	**vii**
Introduction	1
CHAPTER 1 Free Yourself from Status Quo	7
CHAPTER 2 Risk, Discipline & Mistakes	21
CHAPTER 3 Strategize to Maximize	31
CHAPTER 4 Millionaire Mentality	39
CHAPTER 5 Your Biggest Problem is You	53
CHAPTER 6 Truth Bombs	75
CHAPTER 7 The Good Stuff	85
CHAPTER 8 Legacy	105
Appendix	**109**
Recommended Reading and Resources	**133**

ACKNOWLEDGEMENTS

I want to acknowledge the one person who inspires me relentlessly. To my wife Andreea, you are my rock and you are my queen. I've never met a person who is more dedicated, supportive, loyal and trustworthy. I cannot begin to describe how much I love and admire you. We are the "A team". You are God's greatest gift in my life. I'm honoured to be your husband and together we will accomplish amazing things.

I want to thank my two greatest mentors. Mark Evans and Chris Rood, you have impacted me immensely. Without you, I would not be where I am today. You have both pushed me to become a better version of myself and to become a better business owner. Thank you!

I want to recognize my co-author and friend Dr. Elizabeth Wallace. You've taken my story and created a masterpiece. I'm so thankful for your insight and brilliance. You are amazing.

Finally, I want to thank my Forte family. Vini, Kellie, Dave and the rest of my team. You guys are my family and you are my friends. Every day we go into battle and fight for results. You inspire me to be a better leader and you are all rock stars. Keep pushing and stay focused.

INTRODUCTION

In order to understand my journey, you need to understand the beginning. It's usually the beginning of every story that shows what each person's challenges and aspirations are, and what compels a person to succeed.

My parents' story, and my own childhood experiences, stayed with me as I grew up and found success in the world of real estate. The story of my journey shows that it's possible to move from communism to capitalism and to acquire wealth and recognition in spite of all setbacks.

I was born in the communist country of Romania. Very few people in the west understand what life was like there in the 1980s. My parents were Christians at a time when political opinions and freedoms were subdued by the "hard rules" of a communist dictator and suppressive ideology that was forced on our people. You see, no one raised in this type of society, especially someone creative or imaginative, could ever be truly happy or fulfilled.

My parents were extremely brave and knew that God had bigger plans for their lives and the lives of their children. My parents are what I consider real entrepreneurs. Not in the conventional sense of today's social media definition, but in the sense that they were enterprising and willing to take risks. My parents desired to pursue freedom and they were willing to create a new life, with opportunities to achieve their ambitions. They were forced to make extremely difficult decisions in pursuit of a better future.

One fateful night, they decided to join a caravan that was attempting to escape Romania and flee toward a new life. Among the anxieties of numerous what-ifs, one concern was dominant. You see, they had five children, but only two sets of arms. As an adult now, I can only imagine the conversation that my mother and father must have had. How do you choose which children to take and which ones to leave behind?

In such a difficult situation, there is only one comforting fact—the idea of faith. Faith was the ally that gave them the courage to act. If not for faith, and a sense of despair for their children's future, my parents would have simply accepted living under a tyrannical regime, given into the peer pressure, and embraced the communist way of life.

With support from my mother, who was pregnant at the time, it was my father who carried the brunt of the responsibility for decision-making. My father was a young man of great conviction and courage. He didn't hesitate, even though he didn't have all the information he needed. He didn't seek the counsel of his friends, and his resolve was unshakeable. He just took action and stopped asking, "What if something goes wrong?" Rather, I imagine him saying in that moment, "What if I succeed?"

How was this man able to make these decisions under this extreme pressure and stress? And can you imagine for a moment being in his shoes? The essence of this book is to use the experiences of my parents to help you understand what drives your own decision-making and what might be the impact of the actions you take. Thinking about their journey will put your own path to wealth and success into perspective.

You see, there is a secret formula for creating wealth. Although there are many paths to making money, too many people don't ask the right questions. Too many people follow the status quo and follow the herd. And the truth is that herds get slaughtered. Too many people live in a free country but stand in breadlines, just like our family used to.

I want to share what I learned from my childhood so that you can learn too. The goal of this book is to encourage you and help you understand that nothing can stop you from achieving self-actualization and financial success, as long as you stay consistent, remain faithful, and never stop pushing. It is possible for you to overcome the kinds of barriers our family faced, to thrive in the new place you will create for yourself, and to have more than enough bread for your loved ones and others you want to help. There are no barriers that you can't overcome.

THE LESSONS I WANT TO SHARE

This book is designed to inspire and offer guidance to people who are ambitious, entrepreneurial, eager to learn, and determined to produce the kind of results that I've been blessed to achieve.

There are many steps and strategies that are essential for reaching your goal, and I want to help you understand those. In our family, it's a given that we help others and so I want you to benefit from what I've learned.

Building a new life is not for the faint-of-heart, so I'm assuming that you have the kind of commitment and "true grit" that you'll need. I'm writing this book for someone who is just like I was when I first found my way into real estate and needed clear no-nonsense advice. If that's you...then keep reading.

THE ORGANIZATION OF THIS BOOK

I'm offering help and advice in three parts, which I hope will make things easier to follow:

Part I helps you to prepare for the journey you're about to begin. I pose some questions for you to ask yourself, to see whether you're ready to travel the path to success. The questions pinpoint the kinds of resources, planning and personal strengths that you'll need to reach your destination. I tell stories from my parents, in their own words, to illustrate and explain the reasoning behind my questions. If you find that you don't have answers yet, don't worry. Using the curiosity and sense of purpose that made you pick up this book in the first place, you'll find the answers. My message is that you have to spend time preparing for the adventure ahead, and my questions should help you to understand what you need to do first.

Part II describes my own journey—literally from rags to riches. In Part I you read about the four-year-old boy who ran alongside his mother and father for days, through cornfields and across ditches, in the dark and drenched by the rain, in order to reach a new life. That boy was me. Those experiences fueled my determination to take advantage of everything Canada has to offer. In this part of the book, I explain the steps I took as I built my business, the problems I encountered and the challenges I overcame. I describe my journey in order to help you to avoid the same traps and minefields that I had to navigate. You'll no doubt face different barriers from the ones I had to overcome, but my lived experiences should make your path a little easier.

Part III sets out my rules for success. These are "musts" if you want to follow in my footsteps and achieve the same results. I've developed these rules from listening to the stories told by my parents, as described in Part I, and from my own journey as outlined in Part II. These rules are the foundation for everything I've done in the past ten years, and I'm passing them on to you now. You'll see that Rule #1 is: There are no rules! But, in fact, I've made up some rules that work for me. Consider them carefully. Ignore them at your peril. Use them as the basis to develop your own rules.

CHAPTER 1
FREE YOURSELF FROM STATUS QUO

This first part of the book is based on nine questions that I use to mentor people who want to achieve success. My questions will help you decide whether you're ready to take the steps I suggest and to learn from me. Being prepared is essential.

The story that my parents tell about escaping from Romania has many important lessons for anyone who is getting ready to make big changes and achieve life goals. Their message is as important as my own, so take time to find out about their journey...and mine.

1. WHAT DO YOU WANT?

[Dad] We were born in Romania, and as Christians in a Communist system, we could not enjoy the freedoms of the secular society. We were limited in what we were allowed to do. I was not accepted to university. I could not have a passport. No freedom. No freedom of expression. No freedom of speech. There was no future to develop anything. Couldn't dream or plan. Couldn't do what was good in the sense of developing me, my family, my children.

> *I thought: "What are my children going to do in a society like that? I have five children—what are they going to do? There must be something better, beyond the country, someplace else."*

It's clear from the story they tell in their own words that my parents wanted freedom. They wanted opportunities for themselves and for their children. Do you know what you want?

Is freedom your goal too? Even if you don't live under a capitalist system that restricts everything you do, perhaps there are other things holding you back—imprisoning you. For example, are you stuck in a job with no chances of promotion? Do you want to run your own business but don't know how to start? Have you tried other kinds of work and decided that real estate will bring you the most success?

Before you begin to make changes, think about what you don't like about the life you have now, and how you'd like things to be in the future.

Making a checklist of the things you want to change will keep you on track. There's no point in making a big upheaval in your life if you're going to end up with the same kind of frustration and disappointment that you have right now.

2. WHY DO YOU WANT IT?

> *[Dad] But on the other side, there was the future that's open. The endless possibilities. The dreams that could come true. The furthering of our lives with the children.*
> *[Mom] So, I thought we'd go to Canada where we would be free to speak, even if we had an accent. We would be welcome in that country.*

> *I would be able to raise the kids to get good jobs, [get] a good education and to like the country.*
>
> *And then we applied to immigrate to Canada because in Canada it's not citizens here and immigrants on the other side. We're all immigrants. We wanted to come here because we have family here but still wanted to be free, free from everything. And then, we could help our family over in Romania.*
>
> *We came to Canada to be free and honest and to work to help other people. You live not just for yourself, but for others. You live to help other people. Whatever they do, you help them.*

Are you just greedy? Greedy to own more stuff just for your own sake?

Or, are you hungry? Hungry for more satisfaction in your work? Hungry to make a difference in the world and to be recognized for how you have helped others while you work towards success?

My parents realized that there had to be more to life than just existing day-to-day. My father was an electrician in Romania and earned enough to buy basic needs. However, he and my mother had a vision of a better life for their children, and they were ready to pay back and pay forward what they gained when they moved to Canada. As soon as they were able, they started helping other new immigrants and sending money back to family in Romania.

When your WHY is so huge that it affects the next generation, you will climb over any mountain to succeed. Your WHY has to be bigger than yourself and your basic needs. I'm serious here. If the only reason you want to be successful is to buy a car, a house or to serve your own needs, you will NEVER truly be successful. Even if you make money, you will be empty.

So, search deep and find your WHY... And once you discover it, ingrain it into your subconscious.

3. WHY DON'T YOU HAVE IT?

[Dad] (Under the Romanian communist system) Bucharest was the centre but then everybody was organized and they took over the offices, they took over everything, [even]the stores. They confiscated from the Jews and from the rich people. Everything became governmental. They took the factories, they took the stores, they took the fuel and animals.
I could not have a passport.
I could not apply to visit anywhere outside Romania.
Society was so limited. The economy per person was very low. The food in stores was limited and there was no freedom.
Society was controlled. And a controlled society is corrupt. Corruption is a result of everyone being afraid of everyone else. So, they had to lie, hide and manipulate. We couldn't go on with that corruption.

What has stopped you so far? Why haven't you already achieved what you've always wanted?

If you look at the story my parents tell, it's obvious why they couldn't achieve what they wanted in Romania. Under that communist regime, there were barriers that placed limitations on what they could achieve. You probably don't face the same external barriers, so what's holding you back?

You and I were not born with a silver spoon in our mouths. Many of us come from oppression, discrimination and extremely humble beginnings. You might have been born in that environment, but you do not have to be a product of it. It's your choice to step out of your current situation and choose more for your life.

4. DO YOU HAVE AN EXECUTABLE PLAN?

[Dad] It was an excellently planned exodus. We gathered together 41 adults, 11 children and 2 leaders for the group. It was very well planned.
We started at 2:30 p.m. going towards the corn plants. By 9:30 p.m. we were gathered there. And we got up, crossed the road and started to run towards Yugoslavia.
And there was a bus station and we could see people at the bus station waiting for a bus to go to work. And our trip was so well planned by our leaders that we just hid behind the bus station in the corn plants. And in about two minutes we saw a car coming—a Mercedes.
It came, made a U-Turn and stopped right in front of us.
The leaders put us in one of the cars—my wife, myself and the three children. And they drove us for seven to eight hours until they dropped us in the forest, where we stayed for the rest of the day.
In the evening, VW mini-vans arrived and we were packed in them. Escorted by the leaders in high-powered cars, we drove until about 4 o'clock in the morning, when the mini-vans dropped us near the Austrian border.

Before my parents could flee the country, someone had to plan the escape with great precision.

My father describes the plan to escape Romania as excellent. As you can see, every step was well thought through and interconnected. As my parents describe it, it was more of a jigsaw than a linear path that would take them directly to their destination. There were several key elements, such as secrecy, the leaders' familiarity with the border patrols, and good timing.

It's not likely that you'll need the same kind of plan as that group of Romanians who were escaping from their communist homeland. But your success still depends on a good plan.

For example, have you thought ahead as my father did about how to avoid causing difficulties for your friends and families? How are you going to transition from your current employment into something new? Have you set aside money to cover expenses in case there's a gap in your earning power?

And, are you ready to write down your plan? It's not enough to simply create this plan in your mind, you have to write it down. Until you've taken the time to write it down, you're just kidding yourself. You will never execute a plan that isn't clear in your mind and clear in writing.

5. ARE YOU READY TO FULLY COMMIT?

[Dad] We decided to leave Romania.
The only way out of the country was illegal. The legal way was denied.
I could not get a passport so I had to do it illegally. And the risk was huge.
My wife and I, we talked, and we decided to go.
But the maximum we could take with us was three children. The people who were going to help us with the trip told us that we could not run over the border with five children. Even three was extremely risky.
More not (was impossible).
And on the day that we planned to go, to leave the country, I took

the two children we were going to leave behind to the neighbour, our best friends. She used to babysit the children, so I talked to her briefly, telling her we're leaving the country.

And one of them looked at me and said: "Dad, wherever you go, don't stay long, because I want to go home."

And it broke my heart. I just started to cry inside and outside. And I just closed my mouth and turned around and looked at the lady. And I said: "Please. Take care of my children."

And I closed the door and ran down the stairs.

I didn't tell my wife what our son said. We just packed. We grabbed the children. We closed the door of the apartment. And everything was just left behind.

Are you ready to pull the trigger?

My parents were in their late twenties when they made the hardest decision of their lives. They had been preparing for almost a year before they made up their minds to escape from Romania. Their decision affected not only their own lives but the lives of their children and other family members and friends.

My parents didn't hesitate to move forward with confidence. Once they had a clear plan and the right people in place to help them escape, they moved forward in faith. They didn't question the plan, they didn't simply "test the water." They jumped in with both feet.

Are you caught up in a need to analyze every little detail repeatedly? This is called analysis paralysis. Are you so afraid of making mistakes that you are over-complicating the decision-making process? Is there a risk that you'll never take action?

Although it's not likely you'll have to face the same kind of life-or-death situations my parents faced, you have to show the same commitment to making a decision that they did. Confidence in making difficult decisions is important if you want to build a business. What you decide to do will affect how successful your ventures will be.

6. HOW WILL YOU MEASURE YOUR PROGRESS?

[Dad] We started running at 9:30 in the evening and we were running all night. All night. Ditches and corn plants and crossing the fields. Just running with one child in my arms, and my wife had the other child in her arms. Then we crossed the border [into Yugoslavia] and we kept running. We kept running and running because we didn't want to stay close to the Yugoslav border.

In the evening they drove us through the night and dropped us at an abandoned crossing on the Austrian border.

This time the crossing was easy . . . we just crawled under the barrier and then we were in Austrian territory.

My mother and father measured their progress one step at a time. Their success depended on how far and how fast they could run. As a four-year-old trying to keep up with my parents, I had no way of knowing where we were going or when we would stop running.

I was just a kid. I couldn't make plans and I couldn't measure the results. You, however, are a grown-up. You can plan, execute and track progress. You can set goals and measure your progress along the way.

Most people fail to grow because they fail to get organized. It doesn't matter how you track your results so long as you measure consistently.

BENIAMIN MURESAN

How you choose to organize your thoughts and actions is up to you. It's impossible to grow if you don't. Save yourself the endless drama and just take my word for it.

If you're serious about growth that starts with the end in mind. Start with your why. Start with having a huge goal, and then reverse engineer the steps in achieving it. Anything less than this will prove to be a waste of your time and expectations.

7. WHAT HAPPENS IF YOU FAIL?

[Dad] Many people were leaving and they were caught. Many were killed. They were drowned in the Danube river. Just horrible.

The jails were full of... they called them political prisoners because they said they revolted against the party and the leadership.

So many people were killed. We couldn't turn back. It was very risky. We had to go ahead, but it was very, very risky.

If the Yugoslavian border patrol had caught us, they would have returned us. We didn't want that because that's the worst disaster that could have happened to anyone.

The organizers were two brothers, 23 and 24 [years old]. During one of the trips, one of the brothers was caught and was in jail in Serbia. So then, his brother posted the bail for him, like $10,000 [dinars]. He got him out on bail and of course, he never went back.

The leaders said: "Stop!" We dropped on our bellies and just waited to have the leaders explore the situation at the border where the patrols were and the observation towers. And they made sure that the dogs were not there; And grenades or any ground that was mined. If we stepped on something a rocket would go up and we would be caught.

Failure was not an option for my parents. They conditioned their minds to succeed at any cost. They were willing to take massive risks in order to pursue a better life. If you make a decision to live by faith, you too can condition your mind to accomplish astonishing things. When all other things fail, faith gives you hope to carry on.

Like my mother and father, for me, failure is NOT an option. I may get knocked down, but I will continue to rise against oppressors and continue to aspire for more. If we don't stand up and create the opportunities we seek, who will?

That's how I think. And it's what my parents thought as they risked everything. What about you? Is failure an option you would even consider? Or do you have a Plan B in case your plan to be successful in your latest venture doesn't map out?

Let's be sensible. If you have a family you want to look after, or if you're using borrowed money on a strict timeline, you may have to be prepared in case things go sideways. But decide now what the chances of failure are and think hard about what you are ready to do, no matter the outcome.

8. HOW WILL YOU KNOW THAT YOU'VE HIT YOUR GOAL?

[Mom] And I remember after about two hours of driving in Austria they said: "You are free." And everybody started cheering and crying and praying. Because they said even if they catch us now you are free. We had left on Friday afternoon and we reached Vienna on Sunday morning. They said we would never be sent back to Romania. We were free. And they dropped us at a UN Refugee Camp.

When my parents arrived in Vienna, they had achieved the first concrete goal they had set for themselves. They were welcomed, settled in a refugee camp, and provided with shelter, food, and clothing. Even though they had to stay in the camp for a short time, they had accomplished their goal and had arrived in Austria.

Likely, your goal is not to find your way to a refugee camp or to reclaim children who had been left behind, but rather to gain financial freedom. Do you have a vision of becoming financially free? Can you see it in your mind? If so, GOOD! Step one is complete.

Now it's time to do the work. I've been asking questions to help you prepare for those steps, and you may already have some of the answers. Here's one more to think about...

9. ONCE YOU SUCCEED, WHAT THEN?

[Dad] When we reached Vienna, I was dropped at a church. I was hoping that one of my brothers-in-law would be there who was already in Austria and I would get some help. It was Sunday night, and that night we slept in the church because we didn't have anywhere to sleep. There was only one bed and they gave us the bed.

We went to the refugee camp the next day and our refugee brothers, the Romanians, received us very well and were very supportive. Some of the men who were missing their families gave my oldest son some money for passing messages, and they called him the banker because although he was under five years old, he was making money.

The Austrian authorities were very nice. They respected us. They saw my wife was in short sleeves and a lady walked into the office and got her a beautiful coat. We were shocked because now to be Christians was something to be valued and respected, and trusted. We were used to being pushed away, marginalized, rebuked and called stupid. So, we had our first experience with the refugee camp. The food, the acceptance, the people were very nice.

[Mom] I remember I went to the hospital to give birth to the sixth child. When I came home the same day, I saw someone coming to the house with more kids. When I looked at them, it was my own kids! It was the best day in my life to see all the kids together.

[Dad] We had three kids in the morning, and then in the afternoon you came home with the baby, and then in the afternoon your brother came from Romania with the other two, so we had six children in the evening! Canada was a new start. We came here with nothing but six children and some luggage. We started right from the beginning with no English. When we landed in Toronto, I didn't understand a word around me. So, then we all started fresh.

What an achievement! My mom and dad had escaped from Romania and were reunited with the two children they had left behind. They were delighted to be free, and they could have stayed in Austria, as many of their friends and family decided to do. But they set their sights on another goal—immigrating to Canada. And they did that too!

One of the secrets of their success today is that they didn't stop once they reached their first goal. They didn't settle for "good"—they were pursuing "great". And that's the secret of my success too, as you'll find out shortly.

What about you? Will it be the end of your journey once you reach your first goal? If you set your sights on earning a million, are you going to put away your calculator once the screen shows six figures?

If so, my message is not for you. You'll probably be happier with one of those "get rich quick" books that you'll find on every bookstore shelf.

This book is for people who are committed to an ongoing effort, who are looking long-term, who will set out for the next mountain peak as soon as they catch a glimpse of it from the top of the first hill.

If this is what you want, then keep reading.

CHAPTER 2
RISK, DISCIPLINE & MISTAKES

The questions that I've posed so far are, in my opinion, the heart of creating wealth. Unless you're prepared to answer them, you're going to waste countless hours and encounter unnecessary frustration. I wish that someone had guided me through this thought process when I got started.

I shared the details of our family's escape for a couple of reasons. I want you to understand that it takes massive faith and determination to accomplish anything meaningful in life. I also want you to understand that there are significant similarities between escaping oppression and escaping the dead-end paths to wealth accumulation.

There are many similarities in the mindset of a four-year-old boy escaping oppression and a young man trying to grow his personal net worth. I think it's important to consider the steps that I took to accomplish both.

So now I'm going to share with you my story of how I used the same principles I learned in my childhood to build a successful company in Canada and become a millionaire at the age of 30.

We're going to dive into the failures and also the successes. I'm doing this because I want to give you perspective, so you understand what it's going to take for you to do the same. It's not easy, but it's worth it... so read on!

RISK

What is risk? What does it mean to you? Have you ever written this question down? This is such a personal question and most people don't ever take time to answer it.

I've realized that we all perceive the idea of risk differently. Every one of us creates stories in our mind and, based on the narratives we create, we develop a thermostat for assessing risk.

The reason why personal development is so critical to financial success is because developing our minds to better assess risk will allow us to benefit from opportunities that other people will completely avoid.

For some people, buying a rental property is risky. They're afraid that they will risk their hard-earned money, risk their time and risk their energy on something that doesn't justify the return. On the other hand, I believe that putting your money in the bank is risky.

And it's risky because the money is dying. Your money is eroding away, year after year, as inflation eats it up. The bank understands the risks, which is why they give you 1.5% ROI (return on investment) on your money, while they loan it out for 18% on a credit card.

> **The first step towards growing your wealth is to evaluate your idea of risk.**

Once you know where you stand, you need to start increasing

your financial IQ and start looking at risk very objectively, instead of emotionally.

Back home in the midst of communism, we didn't have any opportunities to start a business or develop. And if one took a chance and owed money, the consequences were severe.

In Canada though, the system allows you to take risks and gives you multiple chances to try again. Although the worst-case scenario here is that you'll go bankrupt, the truth is that you can start again in a few years.

It's like losing at a board game, then being allowed to start over again. To me, it's amazing that more people don't understand this concept. They're scared of doing anything more than going to a job and barely getting by which, in my opinion, is the riskiest thing that a person can do.

FINANCIAL DISCIPLINE 101

For the first seven years of our marriage, my wife and I adopted a frugal millionaire mindset. We budgeted every penny and saved half of our combined income. Fortunately for us, my wife's parents taught her how to save money, so it wasn't a struggle for us to live way below our means.

"Spend one, save one" was our philosophy.

My income was spent on living expenses, and my wife's income was going into our savings account. We were under the belief that we could save our way to wealth. The ability to save money seemed to be the superpower of successful people. We read books like *The Millionaire Next Door*, which glorified frugal millionaires.

We delayed our gratification by driving old cars and living in a rental apartment. I look back on that time and call it the "Period of Discipline." We didn't have a specific plan, but we were saving money until we found the right opportunity. This experience was very valuable because it forced us to develop responsible money habits.

The other benefit of this lifestyle was that we didn't stress about money. I could manage my cleaning business, while my wife had a steady income from her job. This allowed me the flexibility to read, study and keep learning.

If you plan on growing your wealth, you have to develop this level of discipline. With enough action, it's not hard to make money, but most people fail to develop this discipline and end up wasting opportunities foolishly.

In a way, the scarcity mindset we developed under communism actually helped us. It helped us understand that massive consumer spending was foolish and that we didn't have to live like the Joneses to be happy. I became fanatical about saving. We did the math multiple times per week on how long it would take to make a million dollars. We spent countless hours watching HGTV and counting our money.

If I were to go back and do it again, I wouldn't waste so much time counting our pennies, but instead, I would focus on making more dollars while being prudent at the same time.

THE FIRST GOOD DEAL

In 2009, our economy collapsed. The global real estate bubble just burst and somehow found its way to Canada as well. My wife and I owned three duplexes at the time, and because we had saved most of our income, we faired better than most people.

I'd been studying real estate investing for a couple of years via courses and books before this all happened. So when it did, I realized that a buying opportunity was on the horizon.

I'd scour the market daily to see what new listings would hit the market. I found a small house in a rough part of town being advertised for $29,000. By my calculation, this house was worth closer to $75,000 if it was in decent shape. I investigated further and found out that a lady had passed away and her home was in the possession of the bank. The bank was looking to fire sale the property to get rid of it quickly.

I had my father's instinct—I didn't stop to dwell on the negative consequences. Instead, I took action, got informed and made my move.

I had just read the book *OPM*, by Robert Kiyosaki, and I was trying to understand the concept of using OPM (Other People's Money).

That's when I had a thought: Could I borrow the money from one person to buy the house, then use the labour of another person to help me renovate it? These were powerful questions. Up until this point, I had done most things on my own. This idea of leveraging other people's resources to take advantage of an opportunity struck a chord with me.

I negotiated with the broker and got the deal signed at $25,000. The only people I knew who had saved their money were my in-laws. So, I decided to ask them for a loan. Once they agreed, I asked my friend, Jon, if he would help me with the renovation. You see, I didn't know much about renovating a house, but I took a chance and pulled in some favors.

RISK, DISCIPLINE & MISTAKES

I realize today that the willingness to ask yourself productive questions is one of the most important aspects of wealth creation. Always ask yourself: How can I do this?

That deal helped me fully embrace the idea of OPM and OPR (Other People's Resources). I bought the house and that year we spent Christmas Eve, Christmas Day, New Year's Eve and New Year's Day fixing it up. My parents, in-laws, brothers and friends all pitched in to help me get it ready to rent.

I even advertised the property for rent long before it was ready. I was hoping to find a tenant for Jan 1. Fortunately, I found two guys who agreed to rent it and I struck a deal where they would help me paint the bedrooms for a reduced rental amount. There was a ton of deal-making... and lots of IOUs being written.

I did it! I rented the house on time. I proceeded to refinance the house and attempted to pull my money back out. I had spent a total of $49,000 on the purchase and renovations. Fortunately, the appraisal came back at $65,000.

The bank allowed me to pull out 65% Loan to Value (LTV) and that gave me a new mortgage for $42,250. This meant that I only had $6,700 of my in-laws' money in the property and after paying all expenses, I had a positive cashflow of $250.

This was a HUGE win for me. I learned a massive lesson. I didn't need to have money or experience to buy real estate. All I had to do was find a good deal, then partner with investors to raise the money and hire affordable labor to do most of the work. The power of responsible leverage is the key to creating wealth. Having the skills to manage my own money helped me to be a faithful steward of other people's money.

I didn't need money to create wealth. I just needed access to someone else who had money. The seller didn't care where the money came from as long as the deal closed on time. This ideology and sense of financial responsibility helped me shape my investment career for years to come.

The following year, I buckled down and bought eight more houses. One at a time, I fixed them, rented them, refinanced the loans—and repeated this process. I laboured on these homes with my father-in-law and friends. This became a scalable model.

This strategy is now commonly referred to as the BRRR method (Buy, Renovate, Rent, Refinance). It allowed me to recycle 100% of the money into new deals, as long as I could buy the house and renovate it for less than 65% of the After Repair Value (ARV).

This isn't just a book about real estate, but this idea of using OPM and OPR collectively has really helped me make millions of dollars. This form of leverage allowed me to not only work hard but also work smart.

I found that the smarter I worked, the faster I started growing.

The next point is another example of working smart vs working hard.

STRATEGIC ADVANTAGE

Shortly after I got married, I started looking for ways to make more money. In my younger years, I bought into plenty of pyramid schemes and small start-up companies. I was looking for something more. I saw an advertisement for a stock trading seminar. I was excited and couldn't wait to check it out.

RISK, DISCIPLINE & MISTAKES

I attended a live event for free, which turned into a $500 weekend, which turned into my investing $25,000 USD in a stock trading program. I remember the hesitation in my wife's eyes when I told her that I wanted to max out our credit cards and buy this course. She obviously loved me because she allowed me to proceed, even though it meant getting into debt.

The sales guys were so good at casting a vision of what my lifestyle could look like. All I had to do was "follow the trends". Sadly, this was not good advice. In essence, I was paper trading. Paper trading is the simulation of trading which allows investors to practice buying and selling securities without risking real money. After paper trading for a couple of months, I was eager to make millions.

I decided to borrow $40,000 from my line of credit and began by buying and selling multiple times per day, known as day trading. I started buying $100 positions several times a day. I'd make a few bucks then sell and do it all over again. I thought I had it all figured out. Then I started noticing that I was paying a small fortune in broker fees, sometimes hundreds of dollars per day. I would rationalize it to myself by saying: "At least I'm making money, right?"

I was glued to CNBC most of the day. It was announced that Apple stock was the latest suggested buy. I was excited because this company seemed to be the big winner that I was waiting for. I decided to leverage my money by purchasing options. Since I didn't have enough money to actually buy shares in Apple, I could pay a fee and purchase contracts on the shares. If the stock went up, so did the value of the contracts.

I could make a lot of money by speculating on the direction of the stock. The only problem was that the options that I purchased would expire at a specific date. If the stock shot up while those contracts were valid, I could make a lot of money. However, if the stock went down or stayed where it was, the options contracts would expire worthless and I would lose my investment. Looking back, I see it now as a risky bet that I shouldn't have made.

This is the world of options trading. I was controlling over $300,000 of Apple stock with $30,000 of options contracts. As I was jumping in and out of these contract positions, I was gaining and losing, but trying to be positive at the end of the day. All of the gambling eventually took its toll on one unfortunate morning.

The stock was dropping like a rock and my option values were losing big time. As the expiration date came nearer, the value starting snowballing against me. Moments turned into hours and by the end of the trading day, I pulled the plug and sold at a loss.

I lost $40,000 that day!

I lost my entire investment. What a disaster. This was the hardest and most frustrating day of my life. I cried, I swore, I pounded on the wood table in my office. Angry, confused and broken down, I came to several undeniable conclusions.

1. I couldn't control the market any more than I could control the weather. I didn't have a back-up plan and I lost. I let greed and fear take hold of me and made emotional decisions about money. I realized that I had to become a steward of money and preserve it above all else. Once I lost that huge sum of money, I vowed that I would never forget that pain or anger that resulted from it. This was a defining moment for me because I committed to never being in that position again.
2. I learned to never gamble with OPM. I now owed the bank money, and that needed to be paid back. That meant that

going forward I was going to treat every dollar like it belonged to God. It was no longer my money, I was merely a manager, taking care of it for a greater purpose.
3. I learned to never enter a business unless I had a strategic advantage. If I didn't have a competitive edge, I wouldn't invest ever again. Nowadays, I only invest in businesses where I can control the outcome. I don't gamble anymore.

I made a commitment to be an insider, not an outsider in any investment I'd ever participate in again. That lesson has saved me and made me millions of dollars in the last 10 years. Unless you have control of the outcome and have a solid Plan B, you have no business getting involved.

The truth is: "You don't know what you don't know."

Unlike the stock market, I can use insider information in real estate. I have the inside scoop. I know the neighbourhoods, the prices, the demand, and how the business works. A new investor can't make the same moves I can because I have more information. The kind of information I'm talking about gives you a massive advantage and more confidence over other competitors.

You can build a massive advantage in real estate if you know the right people and understand how the business really works. You can't do that in the stock market and that's why I don't recommend buying stocks, bonds or mutual funds. If your strategy is to invest and pray it works, it's a poor investment. You will eventually lose.

CHAPTER 3
STRATEGIZE TO MAXIMIZE

So pose this question to yourself: Do you have a strategic advantage? Are you the clear winner in your marketplace? It's a serious question that most business owners never think of. The abbreviation that gets a lot of use is USP (Unique Selling Proposition). It's your differentiator. It's the reason why your customers want your products instead of your competitor's products. If you don't have a clear USP, you're not going to grow.

Just like the stock market, people assume that all they need to do is follow the trends. The problem with following trends is that it doesn't work. By the time most people jump on the trend, the real money has been made. The pioneers and innovators of every industry capture the most market share, then copycat companies try to make money by jumping on the bandwagon.

There's an expression you may have heard: "If you're not first, you're last." Unless you have something special that other competitors don't, and can advertise it well enough to matter, then don't follow the herd.

These days, unless I have a strategic advantage, I won't jump into a business. This forces me to stay in my lane and mind my own business.

Minding your own business is a powerful strategy if you want to create wealth.

My father didn't follow the communist trend or follow his neighbours in the breadline. He made a calculated risk, took action and stayed focused on his own lane. Although that stock market experience was extremely frustrating, it helped me become a free thinker. I was no longer going to jump on the trend or follow the herd.

This is a tough subject for me because I see so many people who still follow the herd. It's the theory of critical mass. This means that once everyone knows about it, it's too late. The real money has already been made. I see the "herd mentality", especially in real estate. One investor overpays for a duplex, then another one follows him. It's mind-blowing just how many people are blind to this concept.

I see these things because I am consciously growing my level of awareness.

I'm always asking: "Who's got the strategic advantage here?"

I want to know the angles and who the actual winners are. I've learned that if I can't see the clear path to profit, then I'm acting like every other sheep. And as you now know, sheep get slaughtered.

GREEDY OR FEARFUL?

One of my favourite quotes by Warren Buffett is: "Be fearful when others are greedy. Be greedy when others are fearful." I reference this quote in every decision-making process. I ask: "Who's being fearful and who's being greedy?"

As I mentioned above, when an opportunity reaches critical mass, meaning everyone is talking about it, it's too late to make money with it. The smart investors get in early and position themselves by buying low, then they make a lot of noise. As awareness and demand increase, new investors start driving up the price. By the time the general public jumps in, the price is already inflated and the investment no longer makes sense. And when the bubble pops and the market drops, the general public investors lose their shirts.

Here's an example that I lived through.

Several years ago, the Phoenix, Arizona real estate market had become hotter than their scorching 100-degree August weather. Homebuilders were putting up dozens of subdivisions, and Americans, Canadians and other foreign investors were flocking to this new desert oasis. Investors were piling in, getting low-cost, interest-only mortgages and buying homes that they couldn't afford. They were speculating that the market would keep rising and as a result, they would make money by reselling those properties to new buyers.

The prices were climbing almost $20,000 every month. As the demand was reaching critical mass, people became greedy. Some of them bought multiple homes that they couldn't afford. Then it happened, the real estate market imploded.

Almost right away, people who took out huge mortgages stopped making the payments. The snowball became an avalanche and the whole real estate industry was turned upside down. People who bought newly constructed homes were walking away two years later because neighboring houses were selling for half.

Before the collapse, several people told me how great of an opportunity it was becoming. They said: "Let's go down and buy properties."

However, my previous experiences finally converted into wisdom. I knew that if I didn't have a strategic advantage in that market and it had already reached critical mass, Mr. Buffet would advise me to wait. And so, I did.

After the market collapsed, my wife and I decided to finally go to Phoenix. We rented a car and started sifting through the ashes. Houses that were selling for $180,000 only one year prior, were being auctioned by banks for $60,000–80,000. It was incredible to see these prices. I did the math and realized that I couldn't build a house for what they were selling for. It was then I realized the value of market cycles and how to focus on buying low.

BUY LOW — SELL HIGH

Many of you have heard the idea of buying low and selling high. What does it mean though?

My belief is that the sale price of a property is only relative to where the market cycle is at that time. If the market cycle is at a high point, then I'm reluctant to buy and hold a property. However, when the market has bottomed out, then finding a great deal is considerably more attractive. That's because you can take advantage of a market upswing, which will help you capture way more profit.

For example, when I purchased that first house for $25,000, it was a good price, considering that other homes were selling for $40,000. However, the real value was the fact that I purchased it during a depressed market. As the market rebounded, I eventually sold it for $100,000—a huge profit on such a small investment.

Now if I had purchased the property for $80,000 today, some would consider it a great deal. However, I wouldn't make the same kind of profit, because I'd be buying in the wrong cycle. My point is this: Be aware of what part of a cycle you're in. If you're in at the top, be careful what you purchase and for how long you own it.

I'll elaborate further here because this concept can drastically grow your wealth.

When you buy in a low cycle, such as after a crash, you're buying based on low consumer confidence and a high degree of fear. If a house sells for 30% of the previous price, it has nothing to do with the intrinsic value, that's the value of the building materials or raw land. When the sale price drops, it's an extrinsic indicator. It's basically how people feel about it.

It's the same with the stock market. This is called sentimental analysis. If someone feels that something is worth less, then they're willing to sell it for less. If someone feels that something is worth more, like a precious heirloom, they will hold out for more money. When sellers were in a panicked state of mind and mortgage defaults were rising, they were willing to sell the houses for cheap.

In April 2011, after driving around for a week, my wife and I bought a property for $60,000 USD, cash. This was a 10-year-old house in great condition, located in a quiet subdivision that was previously selling for over $160,000 only a year before. It was an amazing deal.

And I'm sure you guessed it—we used OPM to buy it without any of our actual money. Frankly, I didn't know how long it would take the Arizona market to rebound, but I knew that if I was buying this house for less than the construction price, I would make money eventually.

A year later, we bought a second house for $80,000 in a slightly more expensive neighbourhood. We rented out each house for $850/month.

After a couple of years of owning those houses, the market began to rise again. We purchased those houses at the perfect time, so all we had to do was wait for the cycle to rebound.

While I did make some money from the monthly cashflow, this was never my real focus. I don't believe that cashflow is the goal of investing. I know this is completely against the grain for most investors, but I'm very confident in this statement. Far too many investors look at the positive cashflow and make buying decisions on earning a few hundred dollars per month. This is foolish investing, especially when they purchase homes in high market cycles.

Cashflow alone isn't the goal for me. A lot of cashflow is. Meaning, the cashflow on a few properties is a placeholder for the appreciation that results from buying in a low market cycle. As a result, when those properties grow in value, I sell them, take a huge profit then buy way more cashflow-producing assets. Unless you can make tens of thousands or hundreds of thousands in monthly cashflow, your job is not done. Far too many investors buy a few houses, make $1,000 per month cashflow and vow to never sell them. Those are the same investors who justified buying in a hot market, regardless of price, because the cashflow offset the mortgage. This is a sheep investing in its full glory.

So, let's clarify this further. If cashflow is a placeholder for appreciation, this means that the property's value is based on demand and comparable sales, not cashflow—especially with single-family homes or small multi-family properties.

If you buy during a low market cycle, the fear-based, sentimental viewpoint will work in your favour. You will also get deeper discounts as a result. When people sell during a time of fear, the price drops quickly.

However, when people start buying again and stability comes back into a market, the prices can also rise quickly.

As I mentioned, smart investors don't buy in overpriced markets just for cashflow. Smart investors buy and hold in low market cycles, collect the cashflow, then resell the property in high market cycles for a premium and then start all over again. I know this is contrary thinking to some investors who buy and hold regardless of the market.

If you can master the principle of investing in cycles, you can create wealth considerably faster than if you don't.

So, I'm sure you want to know, what happened with my Arizona properties?

I have only seen the properties physically once since I've purchased them. As you know, I used OPM for the purchases, so I've never had to tie up any money in these deals. Also, both properties have been rented steadily since the purchase dates. Can you guess what I did with both properties? Here's a hint...

In 2018, the Phoenix market was on fire and I was starting to see the same greed come back in the market. Human nature has a way of repeating itself. Now you can understand how the average investor thinks, so you too are gaining a massive competitive advantage for creating wealth.

I've recently sold both of those properties, and in addition to the eight years of cashflow, I've made $210,000 in profit on just those two homes!

Isn't that crazy?

I don't have to guess anymore. I simply focus on buying properties when the market cycle is low and wait patiently for amateur investors to drive up the prices.

Can you guess in which part of the cycle the Canadian market is right now?

Across Ontario, I see the same speculative investor behaviour that I saw in Phoenix. As a result, I've sold over 200 properties recently for massive profits. Buyers are creating bidding wars, sometimes paying as much as $60,000 over asking price. It's incredible to see the same patterns emerge.

I'm truly thankful that I learned my lesson and grateful to have lost money in the past. The lessons that I've learned have truly given me massive perspective and an enormous advantage in this business.

These days, I only invest in things that I understand and things that show a high probability of success.

CHAPTER 4
MILLIONAIRE MENTALITY

After seven years of saving, investing, and learning, my wife and I were almost millionaires. All of our assets minus our liabilities resulted in almost one million dollars of net worth.

BECOMING A MILLIONAIRE

When we were preparing for this milestone, my wife and I fantasized about throwing an extravagant millionaire party. We were going to rent exotic cars, go on expensive shopping sprees, and eat at the top restaurants. We'd been dreaming about this goal for years and we were almost there. This was the ultimate achievement that would make us feel accomplished, finally, and would justify the sacrifices and delayed gratification.

We were sitting on the couch one Christmas Eve doing our annual net worth calculation, and to our surprise, we finally hit the goal. The calculator read $1,150,000. We'd overshot by $150,000. We yelled excitedly: "We are finally millionaires!! WooHoo!" We looked at each other and I asked: "What now?"

What we did next was mind-boggling. Nothing. We did nothing—we just went to bed.

We realized then that the goal of becoming millionaires was simply a mindset. We weren't going to change our lifestyle, our spending habits or our attitudes. It was just a number on a board. That's it. We were just as happy at $50K as we were at $1M. The target was simply a motivator, a driver. It was the thing that got me out of bed on Saturdays and helped me put in those long hours. But once we reached it, it felt kind of empty.

That's when we finally had an "aha moment". We love the game, not the money! The process of reaching our goal was the real reward.

I believe that everyone should aspire to become a millionaire. And not because of what you'll do with the money, but because of the kind of person you have to become to achieve that goal.

The discipline, the control of instant gratification, the commitment, and the attitude of abundance are the most valuable rewards at the end of the commas and the zeros. It's the discipline and gung-ho attitude that can never be taken away from you.

That's why, if a millionaire goes broke, he can make it back faster than before. Truthfully, the real value of becoming a millionaire is that you don't have to worry about poor-people problems—problems like paying bills, buying groceries, and sending kids to private school. Having money really changes your thinking and allows you to focus on bigger things. If I had to start over again, I would first focus on changing my thinking.

You can't become rich until you start thinking like rich people.

And the next topic explains how to go deep on mindset development. It's incredibly powerful if you can embrace this secret early on.

ABUNDANCE — THE WINNING FORMULA

What do I mean by abundance? Abundance is a mindset that isn't focused on scarcity. Developing an abundance mindset shifts your thinking from pessimism to optimism. An abundant person has hope that there's more out there and is always asking questions on how to get it.

There's a massive shortcut that you can take on the road to financial independence. Everything you do and have is the product of your thoughts. If you desire to have wealth, then you first must think like wealthy people, develop their habits and follow their actions.

What's the secret of becoming a millionaire? You guessed it—start thinking like one. Millionaires think in terms of abundance, not scarcity. This might be hard for you to do because so many people in your life perceive the glass as half empty. Millionaires not only see it as half full but then ask themselves: How can I fill it to the top?

Millionaires don't look at problems the same way you might. For a millionaire, a problem is just another opportunity. They see a need in a marketplace that most people aren't willing or able to fill. They are always asking questions like: How can I change this? How can I grow that?

This mindset doesn't come naturally to most people. It requires conditioning. This is a muscle that needs to be developed over time. Although some people are naturally optimistic, this natural talent can only take you so far without daily practice and development.

So the question is if you struggle with abundance, how do you improve? The answer is gratitude.

GRATITUDE

Practicing gratitude opens up your heart and mind to ideas of growth and abundance. In practicing gratitude every day, your brain will re-wire itself and start processing thoughts that will push you to grow. Every wealthy person I know is thankful for what they have and they remain humble.

Gratitude is the secret weapon of the rich.

Plenty of poor people live in negativity, complain all the time and never seem to have enough. Living with an attitude of entitlement or jealousy can never bring you true wealth. Negativity is a poison that will rot you from the inside. You see this with social media "haters" all the time. They're either too lazy or incapable of doing great things, so they criticize people who are winning. This is simply a futile effort to feel important and justify their mediocre existence.

Don't surround yourself with negative people. I don't care if it's friends, family or neighbors. You need to guard your heart and mind from this toxic behaviour. If you don't, you'll find yourself developing these same thoughts.

As I mentioned, wealthy people have wealthy minds. That's a fact. Wealthy people are generous and give value to others around them. I'm a firm believer in the following statement:

Your wealth will never exceed your level of gratitude.

The more gratitude, understanding, and empathy you practice, the more will flow back your way. My pastor once gave us an example by extending his arm out and making a fist.

He said: "This closed fist represents your closed heart. Nothing can flow out and nothing can flow in." Then he opened his hand and said: "An open hand represents an open heart: love, gratitude and abundance can flow out and they can also flow in."

Creating wealth works the same way. If you live with an open and abundant state of mind, you'll give your time, energy and money. In doing so, your heart and wallet are open for people to make deposits back into your life. This is a powerful concept that I've come to better understand recently.

I see many people who are "too busy" to share their time, energy or money with someone whose status is perceived to be less than their own. However, I believe that these small investments are seeds, and until you plant them wisely, you can never bear the fruit that may develop from them. And although not every seed will blossom, you can't know which one will until you plant it.

Recently, I attended a real estate event where a local charity (Habitat for Humanity) had set up a booth to raise money and build a home for a needy family. By the end of the day I walked by the booth and the event organizer asked me: "Would you like to donate to support this cause?" I asked her: "How much have you raised today?"

To my surprise, they had only raised $300 dollars, even though they were offering $900 worth of value to the winner of the auction. I asked how much do you need and she replied: "$700 would be great." I told her that I'd be happy to donate $900. But as I was getting ready to make the payment, I felt a knot in my stomach. I was growing frustrated because we were at a real estate event with hundreds of people, and no one was stepping up to actually help this worthy cause. The attendees were all busy focusing on the free swag bags and 20-minute sales pitches. So, I had an idea...

I said: "I'm making it my goal to help you raise some actual money today." I asked: "Do you trust me?"

She replied: "Yes, what do I need to do?"

I asked her to get on stage and tell the story of the Warsamas family. This family had been struggling to provide for their daughter who had special needs and they had to find a real home. They'd been living in poor conditions and needed better accommodations. I approached the organizer of the event and asked if I could take the stage for a few minutes. I wasn't a scheduled speaker that day, but I felt a tug to do something more. I made it my mission to help.

The woman took the stage. After sharing a heartfelt story about the Warsamas family, she started the bidding at the latest amount of $300. "Can anyone give me more," she asked. Slowly, the audience increased the bid to $475. I nudged the guy sitting next to me and said: "Come on man, you need to do this." He raised his hand and said: "$600."

Shortly after, the bidding came to an uncomfortable halt at $725. The women on stage started looking at me as if to ask: "What now?" I quickly stood up, grabbed the charity branded T-Shirt and walked towards the stage. I didn't really know what I was going to say, but I knew that I had the right intentions and somehow it would be all right.

I grabbed the mic and asked the audience a question: "Who here lives in abundance?" I knew that if I just gave them perspective over how important this family's life was, certain people would rally with me in my effort.

"Who will make an impact in this family's life?"

I explained that I was an immigrant who had escaped communism and arrived in Canada because someone had compassion and empathy towards our family. I asked again: "Who will stand up and live in abundance?"

A man raised his hand and yelled: "$800!" The room was getting tense and the DJ turned on some background music at my request. I asked again: "How can you expect to receive when you're not prepared to give?"

I knew that I had to lead by example in this moment. Taking charge of the stage and asking for money wasn't enough. I had to walk the walk. So, I said:

"I'm willing to match any donation 100% for anyone who comes up to $1,000."

A landlord named Dan yelled out: "$1,000!" Then a local realtor named Aditya shouted: "Me too!" Then a local investor, Theresa, stepped up and within a few minutes, we had raised $5,000 for this family. And all of it because of one thing: Abundance. The audience started to see that the only way they were truly going to grow was to practice giving abundantly.

I was incredibly thankful for this experience because it confirmed my belief that most people are good. They want to step up and do big things. Sometimes though, they need a little nudge, or they need to be reminded of how blessed they truly are. If you can develop this mindset of abundance, it will bring you joy and success for years to come.

A few days later, we visited the office and construction site for Habitat. We were told that they don't get many donations of that size and that they were so appreciative of our efforts. We even partnered with them to spend a day on-site with our entire staff, building this home.

As you've seen, one thing leads to another and living in a state of abundance opens up opportunities to serve and grow in many areas of your life. I urge you, don't pass over this point lightly. This can be a total game-changer. All you need to do is practice daily gratitude and start opening your heart and mind to living in abundance. My father taught me, through his actions, how to cultivate an attitude of abundance and I'm confident that it's the reason I'm here today.

Once you develop this mindset, you'll start to look at money in different terms. You'll start to see that money itself is not the goal, but simply a tool to help you accomplish great things. The next point will help you to explore this idea further.

LESSONS ABOUT MONEY

I'll start with a bold statement that perhaps you're not comfortable with...

Money is a tool. Nothing more and nothing less.

Often, we give money too much control over our lives. We become a slave to what money can do for our lifestyle and our egos and, ultimately, we make money an idol.

You have two options here:

1. You can control money.
2. You can let money control you.

Let's assume that you want to control money. If that's the case, then you need to redefine it in order to help you control and make more of it.

Think of money as a simple tool. There's a vast supply of it out there. Your ability to find it, manage it, and multiply it is directly related to skills, systems, and resources. There are many different ways to manage and multiply money. As you know from the previous chapters, I love using OPM to invest in real estate deals.

I borrow money, then leverage my skills and business systems to multiply it efficiently. I've spent years creating a system so that I can simply borrow more or less, depending on my monthly goals. It's not emotional for me, it's logical. I simply have a better process for multiplying it than the person that I borrow it from.

Other people are good at going to a job, saving money and providing for their basic needs. I spent the last 12 years investing in skills and learning how to multiply money. I've invested hundreds of thousands of dollars in my development so far and I continue to do so. I'm not great at many things, but I've focused my efforts and developed my ability to invest and grow capital. As a result, people want to invest with me.

They partner with me on real estate deals or lend the money to my company for expansion efforts. Either way, my skillset is in multiplying money. Once you train your brain to see money as a tool, you'll start seeing the opportunities. The next challenge is learning how to focus your efforts.

In his classic book, *Acres of Diamonds,* Russell Conwell tells the story of a farmer who sold a very valuable property to search for diamonds in another land. After the new owner purchased the farmer's land, he stumbled upon one of the largest diamonds ever found.

Too many times, we're disillusioned by a syndrome known as "Shiny Object Syndrome". We assume that the grass is always greener on the other side. More often than not, this is a myth.

There are diamonds all around you, if you just open your mind.

I've seen this phenomenon in my local real estate market.

The prices increased quickly in recent years. We're flooded with foreign investors looking for diamonds.

Instead of investing in their own backyards, they came here in search of wealth. They obviously have no advantage of buying here and many created bidding wars in the local real estate market.

During this madness, I started thinking about something that Grant Cardone says often:

"Who's got my money?" This is a powerful question to ask yourself. What he means is: Who can you do business with? Who has resources that you can leverage and make money from? Whenever you can provide value to another person, it's an opportunity to make money. Where are the buyers who have your money?

So what did I do?

I leveraged my resources to create wealth for myself. Here's how I did it:

1. My team used our knowledge to scour the local market and find deals.
2. I used OPM to buy these properties at a discount.
3. I created a website where out-of-town buyers could get access to my private listings.

4. I started selling houses to these investors and built a great monthly revenue.

I was able to do this because I don't think about money the same way that most people do. I see money as a tool that I can bend and leverage to my benefit. I'm sure you're starting to see now that all of these lessons work together. If you can master these principles and know when and how to use them effectively, you can start creating wealth quickly.

You can start today by looking in your toolbox and identifying which of these you can use.

1. Do you have the right mindset?
2. Do you understand OPM?
3. Do you have a strategic advantage?
4. Do you understand how money actually works?
5. Do you know when to buy vs. when to sell?
6. Can you identify greed vs. fear and know how to use them?

Once you can answer "Yes" to the previous questions, the next step is to learn how to become the bank. Learn how to control money at a high level because those who control the flow of money win the game.

THE BANK

Now that I've crossed the bridge of financial freedom, I realize that wealth creation doesn't move in a straight line. Wealth grows exponentially. The main factor that dictates the slope of that growth is wisdom.

For example, you've heard from the Bible that: "The borrower is a slave to the lender." I heard this repeatedly growing up but didn't know what it meant until I owned rental properties. Many of my tenants were great people. I provided clean, safe housing and they paid the rent on time.

One day I was talking with one of my tenants and I asked him: "Why don't you own a house?" He told me that he had bad credit and that even though he made good money, the bank wouldn't give him a mortgage. I struggled with this issue because I thought that everyone should be given a chance to own a home, even if they'd screwed up in the past.

When my father purchased his first home, he barely made enough money to cover the mortgage payments. He and my mother were working two or three jobs to provide for nine children. The bank manager told him to attach a picture of our family to the mortgage application and, miraculously, my father was approved to buy his first home. This early experience made a huge impact on me and it made me feel compelled to find a way to make homeownership possible for other hard-working families.

I decided to find a solution. After months of researching mortgage rules and figuring out how to raise money, I told my wife: "We're starting a mortgage company." I thought that it was either the best or worst idea I'd ever had.

I didn't know how I was going to raise the capital, but I knew that there was a need in my city for mortgage financing and no one was filling it. I also knew that I would create the only private mortgage company willing to help these families. The banks were tough and other private lenders charged ridiculous fees. I'd discovered my "Acres of Diamonds". It was under my nose all this time.

Asking myself good questions, living with an abundance mindset, and being willing to serve people helped me discover this business niche. I bought a cheap house for $45,000, did a complete renovation, and found a great lady who really wanted to become a homeowner. I sold it to her with a seller-financed mortgage. I partnered up with another investor and was able to give her 100% financing. She was thrilled. She now owned a fully renovated house, for only $100 more than what she spent on rent. I was happy with the $357 per month cashflow, and my investor was thrilled with his new private mortgage investment. It was a win-win-win for everyone.

As soon as I completed this deal, I knew that I had a viable business. I was determined to become the largest private lender in Southwestern Ontario. With a fresh burst of energy, I started finding, fixing, selling and mortgaging houses.

Within three years, the market increased, and so did the value of all the rental houses I had purchased previously during the recession. I sold most of them and funneled everything I had into the mortgage company. We hired a project manager to manage the renovations and an office manager to manage the large volume of applications for our financing program. Five years later, we've become the largest private lender in our city.

Our company, Forte Real Estate, has an amazing team of caring, loyal employees and we've had the privilege of helping dozens of families achieve the ultimate dream of homeownership. Forte Real Estate has grown into the largest private buyer/seller of homes and is considered one of the best work environments in our region. We've been incredibly blessed to be in a position to serve so many families at a high level.

Forte Real Estate has committed to making homeownership possible for another 100 families in the next five years. I know that we can reach that goal by maintaining the same integrity, underlying ethical principles, and determination that we have used to get to this point. If you want more information on partnering up with us as a private lender, visit www.fortere.com.

Becoming the lender will give you an enormous advantage in creating wealth. That's because debt and credit are fantastic leveraging tools. As a lender, you borrow money at a low rate and lend it at a higher rate. Your profit is the difference between what you borrow at and what you lend at. This is called the spread. For example, you might borrow money from a line of credit at 5% and then turn around and lend that money for 9%. That means that your profit would be 4%.

This is how the lending game works at a high level. I leverage my lower cost of funds and lend money out at a higher rate. Although it can take years to master this principle and turn it into a real business, it's quite easy to get started.

Banks have been using this secret for thousands of years. Every time you deposit money into your savings account, it creates a reserve for the bank. They pay you 2% interest on your money but then they loan it out at 18% interest, via a credit card. It's the cycle of debt. Once you understand how it works, you can leverage your way into deals. However, beware of the greed monster. As previously stated, don't enter deals where you don't have a strategic advantage.

Leverage can be a powerful weapon. I'll caution you though, this weapon can also be used against you if you're not careful. Next, we'll discuss a fundamental characteristic of wealthy people. It's a state of mind, it's a state of reaction, and it's also a state of curiosity. It's the skill of becoming a problem solver.

CHAPTER 5
YOUR BIGGEST PROBLEM IS YOU

From a young age, I understood that problem solving was an important part of life. Ignoring problems or refusing to deal with them simply wasn't an option. This type of resolve has helped me tremendously as an adult. I refuse to let problems slide. I want to quickly resolve situations as they arise. Some people ignore obvious problems in hopes that they will magically disappear, but I don't. I like to tackle things head-on and fight for what I want.

BECOMING A PROBLEM SOLVER

Although you can't force a solution to every problem, be willing to get dirty to problem solve. It's the key to unlocking new "diamonds" all around you. Being willing to tackle these problems will help develop your creative-thinking muscle. People have said to me: "I'm just not creative." Every time I hear this I cringe. It's just a lazy excuse for not being willing to think outside the box.

You don't need to be creatively inclined to solve problems, you simply need to make an effort. By taking bold action to find solutions, creativity becomes inherent and you develop it, just like a muscle. Nurture dominates nature in this way.

The people who solve problems are the people who win at life. That's a fact. So if you're not creative, then start becoming curious. Find problems that you can tackle and watch the creative juices flow. I don't believe that we were created to be static beings. We were created to be fluid and adaptive.

It's in creation that creativity lives.

Start with small problems, and work towards bigger ones as you become stronger.

I ask myself questions every day, all day. People who are close to me can see when my creative juices are flowing. I'm completely obsessed with seeing the angles and working out the answers. Problem-solving has little to do with your IQ. The reason I know that is because I failed math twice in high school.

If you develop a passion for problem-solving, your mind will start to create conversations and your subconscious will start solving problems. This isn't something that you can force on yourself. You either want to become a problem solver or you don't. You're either naturally curious or you're not.

I have an overactive mind. It's constantly moving. I see kids these days who are just like me. They're failing in school and get punished for not getting straight As. These kids aren't broken, they're bored. They don't care about topics that don't have any applicable value in life. They don't care about theory. They care about results.

With the speed of technology growing, they'll get bored faster and faster. Life moves very quickly now, compared to 20 years ago. You have to stimulate them in order to educate them. I understand them very well. If there's no practical outcome, then I don't want to be bothered. If I see the purpose behind a project and I can get excited, I'm all in.

Give me a subject, like making money, and watch my Einstein mind go to town, baby! It seems as though, as soon as the numbers have a dollar sign, the math is extremely important. So, if you or your children struggle with math, don't worry. Math might not be the problem, motivation and inspiration might be.

The amazing thing about becoming a problem solver is that you identify your worth.

Just like my example of the $5,000 fundraising event, when I asked myself: "What's my value here today?"

Aside from the fact that I wanted to support a good cause, I also wanted to put a dollar amount on what my time was worth. By taking control of the fundraiser, I was able to raise the amount of donations from $300 to $5,000 in 15 minutes. I solidified my value to myself and every attendee that day. They looked at me as though I could print money. And the truth is, I can.

You know by reading this book that I use money as a tool. At the fundraiser, I used my skills of persuasion to create money from thin air. As Grant Cardone says: "Someone has my money." I knew that the audience had the money that this family needed. Someone just needed to be bold enough to ask for it.

Money is a myth. It's not real. It's a set of numbers on a page. Money doesn't have intrinsic value. It's only worth the value that you place on it in a given situation. I used OPM and OPR strategically to raise the money that night for Habitat for Humanity. Let's break down exactly what I did:

1. OPR (Other People's Resources)
   a. I used the organizer to influence the crowd and ask for more money.
   b. Since the organizer had more influence with the audience than I did, her involvement brought a higher level of credibility and awareness.
   c. I nudged the most influential attendee in the room to make a bid of $600. Once his bid was placed, his influence also further cemented the value in the audience's mind.
   d. I asked the audio engineer to play emotional music behind the message, which I knew would evoke feelings with the audience. I learned this from my pastor, Danny Cox, that music has the power to reach the corners of the soul where the spoken word cannot.
   e. I started pointing to other influencers in the crowd during my request for more money. With every "Yes" came more influence with the audience.
   f. We grabbed the hard hats and t-shirts of the charity and brought them on stage to visually enhance the experience.
   g. When the charity spokeswoman told the story about the girl with special needs, it furthered the emotional influence on the audience. They started to become captivated.
2. OPM (Other People's Money)

a. The above uses of OPR evoked so much emotion in the audience that people felt compelled to contribute to the experience and the cause.
b. I used my money to match anyone who would donate $1,000 each.
c. People stepped up and we raised a total of $5,000.

So, how did I raise $5,000 in 15 minutes? I did it by understanding and using OPR and OPM wisely.

Remember, other people have what you want. If you want massive results and want true wealth, you have to master the skills of using OPR and OPM. That's the only way to really scale and compound your growth.

That event cemented me as the biggest problem solver in the room. It confirmed to the audience that I had significant value and I was a person of resolve. Even though I felt great about the result, I felt more grateful for the ability to impact the Warsamas family. You see, you not only have to become a problem solver for your own needs, but you also have to develop this skill if you truly want to help other people.

There are plenty of needs in this world and ever one of them needs a solution.

These principles are very real and extremely challenging for some people. You can really accomplish amazing things if you first develop the right mindset. The next message refers to one of the most critical components in achieving wealth. That component is your belief system.

LIMITING BELIEFS

That story about raising $5,000 for Habitat for Humanity is amazing, right? It sure is, but here is the part where the skeptics come in. Maybe you're one of them?

Whether you're a glass-half-empty kind of person or simply don't agree with the facts, I'm sure you can agree that most limitations in life are self-imposed. Our financial development can never exceed our level of discipline, level of courage and level of resolve.

After studying Russell Brunson, creator of ClickFunnels, I understood that there are three types of limiting beliefs that stop people from taking action. They are: 1) Limiting beliefs about a vehicle or investment, 2) Limiting external beliefs, and 3) Limiting internal beliefs.

Limiting Beliefs about a Vehicle or Investment

This belief forces a person to think: "Real estate doesn't work, or that company is a scheme." They are skeptical because they don't have any confidence in a process or opportunity. The only way that most people get over this limiting belief is by seeing someone else do it and succeeding.

Limiting External Beliefs

Some people know that the vehicle works, but they still hold back because of market conditions or external factors out of their control. This includes statements like: "The market is too hot to find deals", "I don't have that kind of money for marketing", and "All the good tenants already have a place."

Limiting Internal Beliefs

This by far is the most damaging and the most limiting belief. This language sounds like: "I don't have the people skills to negotiate", "This is too much work and I just can't figure it out", and "People will judge me if I buy rental houses."

These three sets of limiting beliefs will hold you back from success. If you struggle with one of these, then you need to challenge it and face it head-on. If you want to overcome any one of them and start moving forward, this is what I recommend:

1. Identify what your limiting beliefs are.
2. Take action regardless of your beliefs. By taking action, you'll start identifying what's real and what's just in your mind.
3. Find a mentor who has done what you aspire to do and ask for help.

Once you see that someone else can do it, you start to feel confident. Perspective is the key. If you were to hang around me and my team for a month and see us making hundreds of thousands of dollars, you would be much more inclined to go home and take massive action. It's fear of the unknown that holds people back. And that's where the power of mastermind groups and personal development coaching comes in.

The following topic is a sensitive one for many people. I've struggled with paying money for coaching for years, but after 12 years and many thousands of dollars earned, I have a greater perspective about the subject.

TO BE COACHED OR NOT?

Just married and eager to succeed, I found a three-day training at a local hotel in town. I talked my wife into attending with me and we were excited. I thought: "This is where I'll find the info and connections that I need to make money."

By the end of the weekend, I had maxed out our credit cards to the tune of $25,000 USD by purchasing a training package that was supposed to make me rich.

What I didn't realize at that time was that not all coaching is created equal! The coaching industry, for the most part, is a money-sucking business. The business of coaching is just that, a business.... The trainers put on a great performance, get you excited, help you raise the limit on your cards, then tap you for all you have. That's the business. I'm not going to pretend that it's OK, because it's NOT!

It's plain greed. If you've been a victim of such schemes then I feel for you—I've been there.

After this experience, my wife and I spent the next two years paying back the loans on our Visa card. It was a tough pill to swallow. It made me resentful of coaches and mentors. I decided then that I didn't need a mentor. I didn't need motivation and hype. I was determined enough to make it on my own. Screw mentors...they were for weak people, not for me.

I did everything myself. I slaved away cleaning carpets, renovating houses, buying rentals and starting a mortgage company. I did this for seven years. I made my first million dollars on my own. I proved that I didn't need a mentor and that I could just figure stuff out on my own. With so much free information online, mentorship was a waste of money.

Then it happened... The Canadian economy was booming and the price of real estate started skyrocketing. I could no longer find deals for my small renovation team. I was stressing out because this was all new for me. I hadn't faced this problem before. I had relied heavily on real estate agents to find me deals, but now the market was just too hot. Business was chugging along, but not growing at a pace that made me happy.

Having heard about Grant Cardone, I decided to attend his 10X Growth Conference. I thought that perhaps I could meet some people who knew how to get me out of this jam. While I was walking around, I spotted a well-known real estate investor named Chris Rood. I recently found out that he had done over 300 deals and I was puzzled. How on earth had this guy done way more deals than I had, and in less time? I had to ask him.

I walked up to him and started poking around for information. Then he said one pivotal thing to me:

"Ben, you don't know what you don't know."

What the hell did this mean? He was saying that I was clueless about key things that would help me catapult my business into the next level. I told him that I didn't need any motivation. I explained that I just needed information and I could figure out the rest of it on my own.

He said: "You need a mentor. I can help you blow this business up." He told me that I was working too hard and that there was a better way of sourcing deals. It was called Real Estate Wholesaling.

Wholesaling is the art of finding off-market deals and learning how to market direct-to-seller, aka, cutting out the agents and middlemen. I started to understand that I could save 20–30% on all of my deals if I learned this method. So after seven years of not needing a coach, I decided to buy a $10,000 USD coaching program from him.

The next 12 months were completely life-changing. We wholesaled and flipped 65 properties, cut 30% of our overhead and developed a leaner and meaner business than ever before. I fully discovered the benefit of having a mentor.

I now understand that a good mentor will help you save and contract time. After this mentorship, I realized that I could have saved years of hard work if I'd had someone experienced guiding me.

An experienced mentor can look at your business through a magnifying glass, understand your limitations and help you overcome hurdles quickly.

I was so empowered by my mentor that I decided to become a mentor also. Chris and I started a coaching company in Canada focusing on providing massive value to new investors, just like Chris had provided to me. We weren't just another company that sold coaching, we were real world practitioners of what we taught. Chris and I understood the game of real estate and practiced what we preached. We were determined to increase the success rate of coaching companies through intentional accountability. We despised the traditional model of most coaching companies, so we completely reinvented our process.

I wanted to use the approach that I had come to acknowledge and appreciate in working with Chris. I wanted to have the same positive influence on younger investors. These days, I'm always looking for more mentors in every area of my life. I know that I can take shortcuts, save time and skip painful lessons by having a trusted guide by my side.

I recently joined a high-level mastermind group. This is the type of group that advanced business owners join to further accelerate their growth. The cost was $50,000 per year. The reason I joined this group was to get access to a man they call the Deal Maker in real estate investing, Mark Evans.

Mark and the other members of this group have helped me scale my business. In fact, it's because of Chris Rood and Mark Evans that I've written this book. They helped me understand that I should share my story and have an impact on other people who are on a similar journey. I'll be forever grateful to both of these men for the massive contribution they have made to my business and my life.

Making money is great, but these days my goals are focused around impact. I keep asking, "How do I help more people in a meaningful way?" Perhaps it's the Christian values that my parents instilled in me or my gut-wrenching commitment to making the most of this life. But whatever it is, I want to inspire and motivate people. I truly want to bridge the gap between knowledge and taking action. I know that with the right information, and by taking enough action, it's not a question of if you will succeed, it's a question of when and how far you can go.

Every successful person I've ever met knows that leaving a legacy and impacting people is significantly more meaningful than just making and spending money.

I decided to discuss this topic because I know that far too many people struggle with it. If you see mentorship as an expense then you will never justify hiring a great guide. If you start viewing it as an investment in your progress, then it doesn't matter what the mentor costs, as long as you end up getting results quickly.

Here's my warning though: Do not hire a mentor who hasn't and isn't doing exactly what you desire to do. There are far too many mentors claiming to have massive success, while the only money they make is from the coaching package they just sold you. Find someone who actually walks-the-walk every day and see if they are willing to mentor you. Be honest—make sure that if they agree to help you, fee or no fee, that you bring your A-game, and work your butt off.

As we grow as business owners, there are always opportunities to help other people grow with you. I'm always looking for hard-working people who have a great attitude. There are more opportunities to make money together than ever before. Make sure, though, that you show up and give it your all.

GENIUS VS. INGENUITY

Sometimes we see a successful person and we think: "That guy is a genius—how did he come up with that idea?" I truly believe that people aren't always as smart as they seem. I think that many people who seem smart look that way because they ask smart questions.

You don't have to be an Einstein to create an amazing business. Ingenuity is defined on Dictionary.com as: "the quality of being clever, inventive or original." This goes back to not following the herd mentality. If you want to be seen as a potential genius, then you need to start thinking independently. You need to formulate your own thoughts and come to your own conclusions.

COPYCATS GET KILLED

If you think that you can simply mimic another investor and make it big, you're wrong. That's because there are many factors that go into a success story. As I said earlier, it's not usually a linear answer.

When I was buying houses in 2009 for as little as $20,000, it didn't seem like genius work. I was buying all the distressed houses because they made sense financially. Once the houses were renovated and refinanced, I collected rent and made a small monthly cashflow.

This didn't seem like genius work to most people. It just looked liked good business practice. No one was wildly impressed with this work—other than my mom! The key was that I kept asking better and better questions as I grew my little business. Every hurdle that came my way, was an opportunity to ask better questions. Here are some examples:

Problem: When I reached four properties, the local bank said: "We can't give you any more mortgages."

Question: How can I get financing from more flexible lenders?

◦ ◦ ◦

Problem: After 12 rentals, the credit union decided that my LOC was maxed (even though it wasn't).

Question: How can I use private money and remove banks altogether?

◦ ◦ ◦

Problem: When I got to $10,000 per month in income, I felt like it was a part-time job.

Question: How can I streamline the process so that I don't have to do all of the work?

◉ ◉ ◉

Problem: I wanted to flip houses, but couldn't find a reliable contractor.

Question: Can I hire a full-time project manager and have him build out a team?

◉ ◉ ◉

Problem: I had a full-time renovation company that was chaotic.

Question: What system can I build to remove the chaos and create simple processes?

◉ ◉ ◉

Problem: I wanted to build a mortgage company, but didn't have enough money.

Question: How can I incentivize other investors to partner with me and create win-win deals?

◉ ◉ ◉

Problem: After 10 mortgage deals, I had a buyer who screwed up a closing, costing me thousands.

Question: How can I structure deals where I don't do any more custom jobs?

◉ ◉ ◉

Problem: After 40 deals, 80% of my staff quit in unison.

Question: How do I rebuild this company, without having to rely on individual employees ever again?

◉ ◉ ◉

Problem: A few years ago, the market dried up and I couldn't find any more properties to buy.

Question: How can I start marketing directly to sellers and cut out the middlemen?

◉ ◉ ◉

YOUR BIGGEST PROBLEM IS YOU

Problem: Once I started to buy directly, I ran into push-back [criticism] from jealous agents.

Question: How can I create allies in the realtor community and build credibility with sellers quickly?

◉ ◉ ◉

Problem: After buying 200 properties, competitors started ripping off my marketing strategies.

Question: How can I enter multiple markets, faster than anyone and create faster than they can copy?

◉ ◉ ◉

The point of all of this is simple—you have to come up against and overcome adversity. If you're copying everyone else around you, you won't gain traction when it counts. By constantly innovating and creating a plan for your vision, you're more likely to succeed because you actually believe in it.

The moral is: Create, don't copy.

I heard a great businessman and founder of Quicken Loans, Dan Gilbert, talk about how you can't achieve anything significant if you don't believe it first. You'll see it when you believe it, not the other way around. I had to envision my mortgage company before I could build it.

After years of creating with ingenuity, solving unique problems and taking massive action, it might look as though I'm a genius. What impression would you have of a 34-year-old multi-millionaire, who owns the largest private mortgage company and real estate acquisitions company in his town?

The reason why I share this with you is not to impress you. It's to impress upon you the truth that anyone who stays committed and focused on creating value will outpace others who lack creativity and try to copy. Take massive action and solve problems that others avoid. As they say...

The riches are in the niches.

To start on this journey, you must be willing to dream big. Dream bigger than anyone else around you. Don't allow negativity or reluctance to take residence in your heart. Although I remain humble and thankful for all of God's blessings in my life, I also remain hungry. You and I are capable of so much more. We simply need to make a choice to pursue it. The only thing holding you back is a decision.

The money follows execution. You can't get paid until you create something worth paying for. That means that once you dream, you need to take action to see it through. Will you fail? Definitely. At least at first. If you get up and keep moving, in spite of the failure, then you have the magic ingredient that all successful people possess.

Don't focus on perfection, focus on progress.

I challenge you to ask yourself: How much progress am I making these days? Are you afraid to fail? Are you copying everyone else's approach, or are you being creative? If you dream big, create your own plan, and execute it relentlessly, I promise that you'll make progress. You'll eventually find that niche or opportunity that will make you appear like a genius. Seek to gain perspective from mentors who have paved their own way. Following this logic can accelerate your growth. It took me eight years to figure this out.

Once I did, I started working much smarter. I had finally created a secret recipe that worked. I was able to insulate myself from copycat competitors and amateur imitators.

Create faster than they can copy, my friends.

I've worked hard for many years, but I have realized that working hard just isn't enough. Plenty of people are hard-working, but they never become wealthy. Working hard isn't the answer, you must learn how to work smart. The stories below prove the massive difference between the two.

Once you learn how to work smart, your life will change.

WORKING SMART

When I started cleaning carpets at the age of 19, I was excited to do every job on my own. If you've ever cleaned carpets before, you know it can be a tough gig. You must carry heavy machines, fill buckets with water, attach extension chords, stretch out the wand, dispense the chemicals and so on.

I used to do gigs on my own. Even though it was easier to bring a buddy, I enjoyed the satisfaction of doing it myself. I kept all the money and I felt great knowing that I could handle it by myself.

I would think to myself: "I don't need someone dragging me down. No one else can do the job as well as I can." Like so many self-employed business owners, I had this mindset and did a lot of work myself. My ego justified this thought process—I had to be a lone wolf and somehow there was honour in doing it alone. This is the same ego that eventually kills most businesses.

In my mind, it was so much easier working alone than dealing with employee drama. Many times, managing other people was harder than just doing the work yourself. I remember being let down by employees who wouldn't show up at the very last minute. I remember having to redo work time and time again after lazy people. When I thought about training employees, it drove me mad. So, the question was: "Is it worth it?" Why not just do it on my own?

I wasn't alone in this line of thinking. In fact, most new business owners start to feel this way. My mother owned a bakery for over 10 years. When she started, she would hire all sorts of people to help prepare the food, serve the food, place orders, etc. For the most part, it went quite well. She had orders, she was making money and the business was active.

But problems quickly started: employees stopped showing up on time, some had bad attitudes, some stole from the register. My mother battled with employees like a disease. After many ups and downs, dozens of employees and years of hard work, she ended up working alone before I finally convinced her to "shut it down".

Today, my main office employs ten full-time people and a handful of on-site contractors. I learned a valuable lesson from watching my mom and from going through my own struggles. The lesson is this: Stop hiring people and start building systems. You can't rely on individual talent to grow your business. It's not scalable. If you can't create a job description, an accountability chart and an easily implemented process, you can't grow.

Think of how many employees McDonald's has worldwide. McDonald's has one of the most efficient systems on the planet. They can onboard new employees quickly and continue growing through organizational efficiency. Do you think they shut down the store when the cook doesn't show up? NO! They simply use the back-up cook. They're trained to operate, regardless of individual talent.

In my life, I try to fit everything into a system. This is critical, especially if you want passive income. If your business lives in controlled chaos, then it will develop bottlenecks of inefficiency.

Working smart is about creating a scalable system.

In my real estate company, we strive for everything to be executed using an efficient process. Every department has its own unique process. This allows us to grow our revenue while limiting the drama. We are a data-driven organization. The last thing I want is drama. We want our competent team to follow a polished and ever-improving process.

It's incredibly hard to convince a small business owner to think this way. It's hard to sit down and write Standard Operating Procedures, especially when your company only has one employee. The truth is though, at some point you will need to, and the sooner you accept this, the sooner you can actually grow a company. Every large company thinks in terms of processes and procedures.

Unless you're willing to adapt your thinking, you will be doomed to a life of drama, inefficiency, and unnecessary frustration.

If you agree with me that you need to work smart, then make the decision to remove drama from your business and life. You must be "obsessed with finding a better way" (Dan Gilbert) all the time. If you centralize your thoughts on this daily, your company will grow, and so will your income. Every day will bring new discoveries, opportunities and insights. Embrace them and make the most of your journey.

Over the years, I've cemented certain beliefs about how to develop a business and how to develop my mind. If working smarter every day is my focus, then I need to build upon the blocks of truths that I've discovered so far. The building blocks ground my thoughts while helping me explore new realities of growth. The next section outlines my undeniable truths.

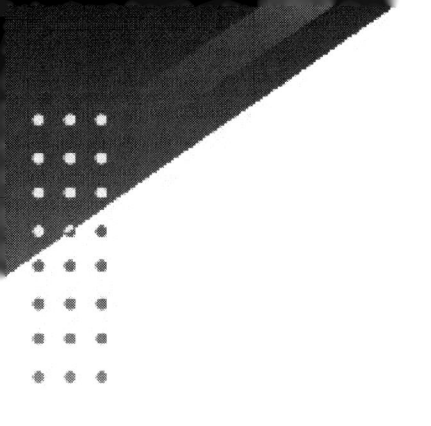

CHAPTER 6
TRUTH BOMBS

I developed the following belief about real estate just before I started buying aggressively in 2009:

> The market is currently depressed and inventory is cheap. If I purchase properties right now, at some point in the future the market will have to rebound and increase in value. I don't know how long it will take or how fast it will rise, but I'm confident that all markets rise and fall.

UNDENIABLE TRUTHS

I was buying houses based on this belief. The reason markets rise and fall is because people are predictable. People become fearful and people also become greedy. When the economy is good, people are encouraged to spend money and enjoy life. That's fine for a while, but people eventually get bored. People are never truly satisfied with how much they have. Once something becomes comfortable, it becomes normal. Once it becomes normal, it becomes average. And once it becomes average, it loses value. And once it loses value, people will want something new.

How many times do you go shopping and see something that you just need to have? This is human nature. It's the aspiration of always wanting more. In a way, it's not a bad thing. It's what keeps you growing. The problems develop when people become discontent and ungrateful.

At this point, we start making buying decisions that go against common sense. We start buying luxuries that we can't afford and start spending money on things to impress people that we don't even like. When spending money becomes a hobby, it gets us into trouble.

After communism fell in Romania in 1989, people started desiring a better quality of life. The people had been oppressed for so long that as soon as no one could tell them what to do, they started spending money. Many of them spent everything they had. It's not that different than here in North America, except they don't have access to ridiculous amounts of credit in the same way we do. We have credit and tons of it.

The problem with credit is that we're borrowing from our future selves.

Every time we buy something on credit, we're making a promise that we'll earn that money in the future and pay for the expense we just incurred. Eventually, this snowball spirals out of control and people accumulate tons of debt that cannot be repaid. At some point, they default on the credit and the lender has to take a loss. When the lender takes a loss, they tighten credit, which limits the amount of available credit, stops spending, then sends the price of everything down. This is the cycle that always repeats itself. It's driven by greed and fear.

When I controlled that Apple stock valued at $300,000, it was a decision driven by greed. I used OPM and tried to speculate on the outcome. In many ways, it's not that different from gambling. I was borrowing from my future self, to make a trade in present time. So, what does this have to do with business?

Well, if you understand that this is an undeniable truth about our market cycle, then you must also realize that there are other undeniable truths, which if understood, can help you navigate through the business of growing wealth. Here are three of those truths to think about:

1. YOUR PLAN WILL CHANGE — ADAPT OR DIE

When I first started investing in rental houses, I had a plan of getting to 100 doors, then living off the rental income. I just assumed that I would capture that mailbox money that we all aspire to have. As the market changed, I realized that I was sitting on equity and since the banks were tightening up, I couldn't leverage anymore. I had to adjust my strategy. I had to modify my plan and start selling some of my inventory to raise money. With new money raised, I was able to leverage further and buy more properties.

Had I not made the shift, I would have lost many opportunities to grow and I never would have realized the mortgage business opportunity. These days, I'm willing to pivot on a dime if needed. I know that being flexible and willing to adapt will help me overcome challenges and take advantage of new opportunities. My lawyer, Paul Brisebois taught me a valuable business equation:

Opportunity = Skills + Chance

Many people have the same chances in life, but they fail to see opportunities that are right in front of them. It's not for lack of chances, it's for lack of skills and vision. By constantly being in a mental state of growth, I'm willing to look objectively at every angle and ask myself: "Is there an opportunity here?"

The world changes so we also need to change. I don't really know what my business will look like 20 years from now, but I do know that it will look different than how it looks today. That's because my business today looks significantly different than it did two years ago. So be prepared to adapt or die.

2. STAY LEAN

While I certainly advocate healthy eating, I'm not referring to your diet here. I'm referring to running a lean business. A lean business is one that doesn't have unnecessary expenses. I'm not suggesting a shoestring budget for your corporate office, but I'm suggesting that you not lease three new vehicles and hire unnecessary staff just because you have the available credit.

Lean companies adapt faster because they're lean. By keeping expenses low and watching your bottom line, you can net significantly more than bulky companies.

There's also a trend among big companies that I'll never understand. When a company reaches a size where different departments have budget surpluses, people start spending more money just to keep the budget maxed out. This means they will spend money unnecessarily, just to prove that they need the same amount for the next year. That seems completely wasteful and ridiculous to me.

We didn't have this luxury during communism. The breadline simply ran out when the bread was gone. We couldn't bake more bread just because we'd eaten it all.

I know of companies with revenues exceeding $20,000,000, who only have a small handful of employees and stay very lean. Imagine a huge bulky boat like the Titanic. It's hard to steer, let alone turn on a dime. I would rather have a smaller boat that can turn easily and avoid massive disasters when the market shifts.

3. GROSS NUMBERS LIE

How many times do you hear someone brag about how many rental doors they have or how much revenue they bring in? I'm here to tell you with great confidence that it's all a lie! Most of what you hear is straight garbage. People always lead with the most impressive numbers they can. It's human nature to embellish the truth. Gross numbers don't matter, net results do.

Grossing large revenue is like being a top-paid doctor. The gross number sounds great until you realize that the majority of their income goes to taxes. They are only left with a fraction of what they earn on paper.

Going to real estate events doesn't help. Investors always exaggerate their numbers to compensate for their lack of results. Many of us feel inadequate or unhappy with our progress, so we want to be praised by others who don't know any better. We brag about the numbers of doors we own or how many houses we've flipped. But most people don't talk about the bottom-line profit.

Gross means nothing — Show me the NET!

If we aim to focus on growth and living a life of abundance, we need to get real with ourselves and look at the relevant data.

Being data-driven keeps you humble. When you lower your ego and portray yourself as less than what you really are, it drives you to grow and drives you to actually achieve the numbers you aim for.

HOW MUCH MONEY IS ENOUGH?

Maybe you've heard people ask this question before: "But how much is enough? When are you going to retire?"

Anyone who asks that question obviously doesn't get it. Business creation isn't solely about making money. The business is a child. Being the oldest of nine children, I could always relate to my business as a child. That's because the business is something that I created from nothing, and my greatest joy is to see it grow.

Just like a child, a business goes through different stages of development, and just like a child, we hope to see the business develop to the point of maturity. It produces a sense of pride and accomplishment to see something blossom and continue growing without our involvement. I like to think of growth in five stages, similar to the development from an infant to an adult:

Infant

When you're just starting, your business needs a lot of attention. And for the most part, you're all alone. You have to meet its every demand and wear every hat. You love seeing your business get healthier every day, but it can be very demanding. There are no days off—you just do what you have to do.

Toddler

Now your business can start walking on its own. You might hire a first employee or customers start calling you for orders. The business is starting to show progress and it's very exciting. Seeing change encourages you to continue pushing it. There's nothing more encouraging than seeing the first fruit of your labour. Even though you're tired, you push on because it's worth it.

Pre-Teen

Your baby is becoming independent. Leads are coming in from clients, money is actually hitting your bank account, and other people start noticing you as a business owner. It feels good to "take a nap" here and there because you've earned it. You're past the initial years of growth. Even though the job is still demanding, and you're still overwhelmed at times, you see progress. The possibility of independence is on the horizon.

Young Adult

This is one of the most exciting parts of growing a business. It's finally independent...somewhat. You have a team that can take care of the day-to-day tasks, but you still have to step in and give feedback. This phase can also be challenging because you're managing people and people have feelings. Managing people and attitudes are now your focus, not just getting the work done. At this stage, you need to grow as a business owner. You have to learn how to become a real leader. This is the phase where you see how mature your business can become.

Adult

That's it—you're out of the business completely. You have a competent team, with great management in place. Your job is to provide vision and build higher-level relationships. This is the stage that every business owner dreams of getting to. It's the stage of accomplishment. Knowing that your baby has become an adult is very rewarding. Your years of effort and work have finally paid off. The business can finally pay you and give you your time back.

So, you can see that it's not about a certain dollar amount, it's about taking something from seed to full blossom. It's about pushing yourself as far as possible to achieve something extraordinary. The real reason business owners keep going is because it's exciting to see your creation develop and grow. It's exciting to see the lives that your creation can then impact and the families that you can employ.

The sense of accomplishment is a driver for most business owners. For me, my passion is to make an impact. I want to positively impact my team, my community, and the world around me. I want people to remember the good that we did here. I want people to be inspired and take action.

This is the reason we work. This is the reason we dedicate our minds to progress. We want to see change. We want to see things happen. We want to see success for our families, friends and neighbours. This constant pursuit helps develop our abundance mindset. And a mindset of abundance is necessary if you hope to impact and inspire other people.

If you really want to take your growth seriously, you need to develop the character of discipline. There's no shortcut here. You either develop the discipline or you will fail. Every successful person I know has created strict habits for their life which propel them forward every day. Although we all struggle with discipline, it's the cornerstone of growth. I'll take discipline over talent any day of the week.

In the next section, I share with you some of my personal rules. I have included them because this is what has worked for me. To me, these are fundamental. Use them as a guideline and adapt them as necessary.

CHAPTER 7
THE GOOD STUFF

Many people want to know the nuts and bolts [rules] of how I invest in real estate and build companies and we'll deep dive into that in a minute. Before I do, I need to offer a few words of wisdom and caution.

ONE

EVERYONE is selling the idea that their way of investing is best. Everyone claims to be a real estate genius and marketing pro. Keep this point in mind: **90% of what you see is stupid.**

It's stupid for so many reasons, that I should dedicate an entire book to exposing this nonsense. There is no best investment option. Only invest in opportunities when you have a Strategic Advantage. I'm hoping that this book inspires you to become a free thinker and invest based on merit, not sheeple guidelines.

Don't you want to win? Well, I do. That's the point of growing a company. I want to win more than I want to belong to a group of "investors" who get together and toot each other's mediocre horns.

TWO

The rules I'm presenting here will work best for you if…

- ✓ You have the same drive and ambition as I do.
- ✓ You've read through Part I and II of the journey and understand the challenges.
- ✓ You're able to commit time and effort to become successful.
- ✓ You recognize that becoming a success takes courage and vision.

So now, let me outline my rules—my guidelines. This is how I invest and grow my companies. I hope this gives you some clarity and provides you with actionable steps to get you started.

RULE #1: THERE ARE NO RULES

If you're waiting for someone to hand you an out-of-the-box business that will make you millions as long as you follow their rules, you may have a long wait. Even though there are tons of such businesses available, and most people dedicate years of their lives and a lot of energy to mastering those rules, the sad part is that the original expectations almost never materialize.

Business is fluid, not static. Just because someone else followed an approach five years ago doesn't mean that you can do the same today. There's no perfect business or perfect business approach.

There are no rules that will guarantee success. There are plenty of good general guidelines, but you have to make up the rules or adjust old ones as you go. Market conditions change daily and the world is ever-evolving. Trying to stay one step ahead of the game is the game.

The example I always think of is the "Real Estate Millionaire". As the market rebounded after 2008, an increase in real estate values quickly followed. Anyone who bought a home in 2009 and held it at least 10 years gained a healthy amount of equity. And if they were smart, they locked in profits by selling to new groups of investors after the rise.

It's easy for those who profited from the market to preach: "Use my strategy!" But what most newbie investors fail to realize is that those market conditions won't last forever. It's a huge game of "Hot Potato."

It works the same way with the stock market. I have a buddy who bought stocks in 2013 and in one year was up over $100K. He thought that he had mastered the market. Unfortunately, the next year wiped out all of his gains, plus more.

Maybe he shouldn't have followed other people's rules.

This is how I stay ahead…

RULE #2: I MAKE UP MY OWN RULES

1. I look for a need in the marketplace. For example, in Canada, there is a massive need for affordable mortgage financing. The banks have tightened lending and many good people can't buy a home.
2. I position myself to fill that need. I started leveraging OPM to raise money and fund mortgage deals.
3. I create a "moat" around my business. By focusing on building great relationships and executing with massive speed, I am first

to market and usually have months of profits before copycats can follow me.
4. Every day I ask: "How can I make this better?" By using this system, I created the largest private mortgage company in southwestern Ontario. With millions of my own money invested, along with other investors, this business continues to thrive today and is still outgrowing any imitators.

Make up the rules as you go. There is no special blueprint. Just find a need, take massive action and work like a beast. For example, another one of my businesses, Lead Ninja (www.leadninja.ca), went from thought to full execution in 48 hours. I put my best people on it, and within 30 days, it was already a profitable business with dozens of new investment partners.

RULE #3: ONLY DO WIN-WIN DEALS

Look, it's much easier to cheat, lie and steal to try and get ahead. Many people do it. But the truth is that it doesn't work. At least not in the long-term. People who take advantage of investors or customers to get ahead will always inevitably fail.

Every time you cheat, you risk losing a relationship. And solid, long-term relationships are why some people win and most don't. For anyone to truly win long-term, they have to collaborate and use other people's resources. That includes OPM, OPR, OPRe (Other People's Relationships).

You cannot win alone. I hear people all the time tell me how they are crushing their competition or "grinding on their own." This is immature and foolish.

In any deal that I'm involved in, I always look empathetically at my counterparts. If I make sure that they're winning, I always find that they do the same for me. It's mutual respect.

Don't make the mistake of thinking that business is a Zero-Sum-Game. No one else needs to lose in order for you to win. In the best companies, everyone wins.

In my companies, I make sure that every employee feels appreciated and loves the working environment. We've helped employees move into new homes, get mortgages, build equity, move kids to better schools, etc. If your team is winning, so are you.

Anytime I hire someone or do a deal, this is my thought:

1. Are we both in the same place ethically?
2. Is everyone winning on the deal?
3. What's the long-term value of this relationship?
4. How can I lead with value to construct a solid bond quickly?
5. How can I impact this person in a positive way?

If I can't answer these questions clearly, we probably won't work together. I live with an abundant mindset. If someone has bad intentions towards me and wants to screw me, they might be able to in the beginning, but they will always lose in the long run. Let me give you two examples.

The Short-Sighted Mortgage Broker

[Ben] Ten years ago, my wife and I were buying our first home together and a local mortgage broker was helping us put together the financing. Two days

before closing, he said that there was an issue with the bank, but he didn't have time to help us find another lender due to some personal financial troubles. We were obviously stressed out, so we agreed to lend him $2,500 to fix his troubles so that he could get back to helping us. We filled out a loan agreement and he helped us to get our deal closed. Everything was fine until it came time to pay back the loan. He never did. He stopped answering his phone, left his job as a broker and never made good on his promise.

I think about this situation because as a young, hungry investor, I told him: "I'm going to buy dozens of properties with your help." Today, I'm the largest single-family investor in my city. He and I could have done millions of dollars in business together ... Was it worth screwing me over for $2,500? Don't be short-sighted. You never know which eager, wet-behind-the-ears kid is going to grow up and become the largest investor in town. Make every deal a win-win and only work with people who share the same values as you.

The Greedy Investor

[Ben] I had another encounter with a local investor who owned dozens of rentals. I called him up one day and told him I'd like to buy every building he owned and help local families get into homeownership through my mortgage company. I told him that we could really help people and make a profit at the same time. He said: "I don't give a S!@# about helping people, I just want to make money!"

We never did business together. He occasionally calls my office looking for deals, but the latest news is that he owes investors tons of money, is

*behind on mortgage payments and business is failing...
I wonder what happened?*

RULE # 4: DON'T FORGET A POSITIVE ATTITUDE IS EVERYTHING

From an early age, I was always curious about the world. I remember always asking "How?" and "What if I did that?" Being curious can be a massive gift.

Today, that same curiosity is one of my largest allies in the difficult world of business. Instead of focusing on the problem, getting angry and becoming negative, I try to remain positive.

I ask myself: "What can I fix? How can I turn this into an opportunity?"

If you ask anyone at my office, on most days I come into work enthusiastically, with a positive attitude, and always focused on winning. This positive attitude is so crucial that most people miss it altogether. So many of them are mistakenly focused on "business"—living within a strict environment of money, rules and blah...blah... blah....

I strive to make work fun. Fun for me, my team, and anyone I encounter.

No one wants to do business with a grump. No one else cares about your woes or problems. They are focused on their own little world. Become a light. Become a positive person that others look up to.

It's not just important for your sanity and health but for your entire team. Investors love people who are personable and easy to talk to. Don't take yourself too seriously. You'll look like a fool.

You can have fun and make a profit. I promise you don't have to compromise.

This is how I stay positive:

1. Regardless of what happens in my business or personal life, the moment I begin to act negatively it gets worse. Therefore, I refuse to allow any negativity or negative energy towards me, even if I have to force a fake smile. My father is the best example of a man who has mastered this concept. He deals with stressful situations working as an ordained minister. As difficult as it gets, he always has a smile on his face. He always has a positive, engaging attitude. I learned how to deal with stress by watching him and it's been a huge blessing.
2. It's easier to be positive when you feel good. I do HIIT training 7 days a week for 25 minutes to release the stress and build up a sweat. I highly recommend that you do the same.
3. Attitude is a choice. I choose my attitude every day. The most important reason I focus on maintaining a good attitude is because it builds character. It's easy to follow emotions and get upset when things go wrong. It's harder to fight through the negative thoughts. That fight, though, is powerful. The moment you can start to overcome your emotions, you can become a problem-solving monster. And solving problems get you PAID.

RULE # 5: FOCUS ON STRENGTHS

Building a business requires skills and aptitude. Growing up, I knew that I had a knack for speaking with people. Watching my father preach from a podium and captivate an audience, I knew that such a skill would come in handy in the long run. I was intentional about building that muscle. Turned out that I was a natural!

I have come to realize that, in business, the winners focus on discovering and using their unique abilities. Meaning, they find what they are good at and only do that. This is a powerful concept because it creates a high probability of success. By focusing on your strengths, and allowing other people to focus on their strengths, you create a synergy of strengths that outperforms any other approach.

Back in high school, I hated math. Actually, I failed twice. Although I've never publicly disclosed my grades before, I actually got a 17% on my final exam. Yes, I said 17%. That's less than an F. I struggled with math because it was not my strength. I played music growing up and have been a right-brained thinker my whole life. I excel at creativity but do poorly with left-brained metrics.

How does a kid who failed math twice end up owning a mortgage financing company, talking about amortization schedules and forecast analysis?

Two things:

1. I take the natural creativity that I have and only focus on building the parts of the company that uses that strength.
2. I find people who are gifted on the analytical side (like my wife) and invite them to add their strengths to mine.

Don't assume that you have to learn it all. You don't. New business owners fall into the trap of trying to wear every hat. I did too. When I started flipping houses, I learned how to find deals, negotiate, perform renovations, do marketing, do bookkeeping and on and on. I thought that's what business owners did.

But now I realize that it's not true. Business owners focus on the activities that they're good at and build a team of rock stars to handle the rest. I've got that kind of a team and business is growing faster than ever.

So how do you find your strengths? Ask yourself:

1. What am I passionate about?
2. What am I better at than most people?
3. If I could look at the business through a microscope five years from now, what would be my role?

When I built Lead Ninja, I brought all of our team into the boardroom. I quickly identified who was needed to get the project off the ground. I asked for feedback to make sure we were on the same page. Then we all dove into our areas of expertise. It was the fastest we'd ever launched a company.

If you own a small business that doesn't operate like that, read Michael Gerber's book, *E-Myth Revisited*. It was my starting point for realizing that I needed to change my mindset and my approach to business.

RULE #6: USE LEVERAGE FOR POWER

The real way to grow anything exponentially is through leverage. This is the single greatest business growth principle that I know of.

Smart investors know that we live in "the spread". The spread is the margin between what you pay for something and what you sell it for. When I think about borrowing money, I always consider the spread. I don't need to have the whole cake—just a tasty piece.

BENIAMIN MURESAN

In real estate, a lot of investors use debt as a vehicle to leverage growth. When done correctly, this is a powerful tool that can really accelerate your growth. But used incorrectly, it's the quickest path to bankruptcy.

A popular strategy is called the BRRRR method. It stands for: "Buy, Renovate, Refinance, Rent, Repeat".

In 2009, following the 2008 housing collapse, I started using this principle to buy houses, and recycle the same money over and over again. Here's how I did it...

I purchased a house for $25,000 using OPM, then spent another $25,000 (also OPM) to perform the rehab. In total, I was $50,000 into the deal. Once completed, I rented the property for $550 a month.

I then went to the bank to refinance the loan. The bank appraised the property at $84,000 and that qualified me for a new 65% LTV loan in the amount of $54,600, less legal fees. I pocketed $53,760.

With the proceeds of the refinance, I paid back my original investor the $50,000 that I borrowed to buy the house and perform the reno.

So, at the end of this cycle, I owned a property that cashflowed $200 a month in rent, which cost me no money of my own.

After doing this, I realized that this was a scalable way of using the same money over and over again. So, I proceeded to buy eight more houses the following year. Just about every month I was buying a new house, renting it out and refinancing.

By the end of it, I ended up with 15 tenants and about $3,000 per month in positive cashflow! Not bad for a 25-year-old, right?

I've used this same approach to create and grow a mortgage company. By understanding how you can borrow private funds and recycle them into new deals, the money is literally endless.

These are my rules for leveraging money:

1. I always have an exit strategy. If things go bad, like a housing crash, I need to know exactly how I plan on paying back investors and keeping their money safe.
2. I always need a positive spread. If I borrow funds at 5% and do a deal where I make 15%, then I NET 10% Profit. That's a healthy spread.
3. I never gamble on deals I don't know. I only invest in deals that I know well and understand the risks.
4. I further secure my investors' funds by controlling multiple ends of the deal. For example, I can buy a house for $100,000, sell it for $120,000, and secure a mortgage asset for the full $120,000. So, I have a $120,000 asset that only cost me $100,000. I know this might sound complicated and to some extent it is. But once you increase your financial IQ, you will start to better understand these principles.
5. I don't borrow money just when I desperately need it, because that puts me at a disadvantage. It's important to be in this type of control. Anytime you're desperate for money, it's obvious to lenders. Make the bank chase you, not the other way around.
6. Pay money back early … not just on time. The only reason why people continue lending you money is because they're confident that the money is safe. Go over and above to guard that money with your life, and pay it back early.
7. Once you know how to leverage money, start leveraging relationships to find more money partners.

If you get good at leveraging money and have built a solid reputation, you'll find that people will be calling to invest with you all the time.

You have to become a responsible steward of money. That's an old Bible term that refers to treating money as though you're managing it for God. Manage it with responsibility and utmost authority.

Caution: DO NOT borrow money if you cannot repay the loan. I'm not an advocate for people who borrow money, then get into financial trouble and end up cheating their investors. You see these stories on CNBC all the time. This, to me, is unacceptable.

When the housing market in Phoenix, Arizona tanked during the housing collapse bubble of 2008, people who leveraged credit had to abandon their homes and equity by the thousands. Regardless of whether money is borrowed from my family or a bank, I always treat it with the same respect. You have to do the same. You can't discriminate between private loans and bank loans. All borrowed money is worthy of your protection.

Using leverage can make you millions of dollars, but it's also a huge responsibility. Before you ever head down this road ask yourself: "Am I prepared to force someone to give up their retirement because I gambled on a deal that I didn't understand?"

I hope not.

RULE # 7: TAKE MASSIVE ACTION...IN THE RIGHT DIRECTION

If you've heard the name Grant Cardone, you know his book: 10X Rule. This man's entire brand is built around taking massive action, and way more action than you'd think is necessary to achieve a goal.

Remember my mother's bakery? She slaved 10 years, 14–16 hours a day, to build a business. She worked harder than anyone I've ever known.

When everyone else was going home, she'd start her second shift. She'd clean and prep for the following day.

As long and as hard as she worked, it was never enough. There were no systems, procedures or trackable metrics in place. It became a labour of love for my mother, instead of a growing enterprise. That little business eventually closed down, at my insistence. You see, you can work 'til your bones bleed, but if you don't make progress, it doesn't matter. Simply working hard isn't enough. You have to build something.

You need to implement systems, hire excellent people, and slowly remove yourself from the day-to-day operations. If you don't, you'll become a slave to your business. I admire my mother for the many years and countless hours dedicated to that business. Watching her inspired me to continuously ask: How can I do it better? How can I help her?

It pushed me to realize that without progress, it's just a job ... it's just a facade. You need to find your niche and you need to build an actual business. If you left tomorrow for 30 days, would your business survive? And more importantly, would it thrive?

Very few people can say "Yes" to that question. They will give you many excuses as to why they are so important to that business. But the truth is that if it's not built to scale, it's not built at all. If there's no process and plan to grow, then you can never truly own a real business.

I started a carpet cleaning business at 19 years old. My first job was to clean my mother's basement carpet. I spent 6 years cleaning carpets, doing janitorial, hiring, firing—and pretending to grow.

As I see it now, that was a failed business. It failed because it did not mature and develop into a real business. It was just a pretend business. Take massive action, but ask yourself: Am I truly growing?

That being said, there is ZERO excuse for not putting in 110% every day.

If you don't, you won't win. Business is hard, it's sacrifice—and it's amazing.

I remember growing up in Canada and my parents having multiple jobs, just to put food on the table. They didn't complain; they didn't give up. Work became so ingrained in their lives and still is, that it's a part of who they are.

This is why you can't compete with the immigrant mindset. There is no such thing as 9–5. It's 24/7 all day/every day. If an opportunity comes up, we go, we work.

This is the hardest part that most people don't get. You can't put in part-time hours and expect full-time results. It doesn't work in fitness, in business, in marriage or anything else.

I now focus on working MUCH smarter and not just harder. However, working smarter doesn't replace harder. The difference today is that I focus only on the highest-paid and highest impact activities. I don't buy and sell houses anymore. I don't do rehabs or paperwork. I don't even go to the closing table at the lawyers. I don't do those things because the business has been built to grow without me.

These days, I spend my time investing in relationships, raising millions of dollars and starting new companies. I'm focused on raising money for charity and giving opportunities to investors who want to grow. But don't think for a minute that I'm not working.

My mentor, Mark Evans, wrote a book called *10-Minute Business*

Owner. Go pick it up. When I first met the guy, he was wearing shorts, smoking a cigar, traveling the world and driving a nice Rolls.

I was confused because the guy didn't look like he was ever working. He looked like he was playing. But he's created a company where the business runs itself while he's taking massive action on new businesses and initiatives. So even though he doesn't look like he's working, he's going hard every day.

My other mentor Chris Rood, who wrote *The Source of the Deal*, is a self-proclaimed mule. He works like a beast. Every day he's working in his real estate company, buying rental properties and growing a huge coaching business.

Everyone I know works like this. This is our life and this is our passion. We love to win and we love to create.

Here's how my mind thinks about Massive Action:

1. I never stop. Even when I'm relaxing, my subconscious is still processing opportunities and coming up with new things to accelerate my growth.
2. I never quit. I've come too far and have been gifted this life. I need to make it count. I'm creating wealth for many generations to come and to impact as many lives as possible.
3. Work is play. I love growth and business so much that it doesn't feel like work. You can't compete with a person who loves doing something and practices every day.
4. Most people want to exist, not thrive. Work is not hard for me if I just stay consistent. If I take enough action over an extended period of time, I can accomplish anything.

If you're afraid of work, you should really consider pursuing a different calling. Business is not for the weak or needy. Business is the toughest game around where most people fail or give up eventually. Most get their hopes up and never truly experience success.

It's absolutely heartbreaking to see someone who has big dreams work their whole life and never reach the goal.

But here's the cool part. Building a business is the greatest feeling you can experience. It's thrilling, fulfilling and powerful if you truly understand the journey and put in the massive amount of work necessary.

RULE # 8: REMEMBER THE PURPOSE

So, the question is: How do you determine if you should go down this path?

Here's what I've found. If you have a massive purpose, then you can overcome any barrier or struggle. If you're only doing it for the money, you'll eventually fail.

The purpose has to be greater than just money. You see, money is a by-product of living with a massive purpose. Your vision for your life has to be bigger than just your basic needs. Otherwise, you'll find that you've spent your whole life chasing money and end up a miserable old person.

You should start with purpose! Why do you want to build a business? What are you going to do with the money?

For me, my purpose is founded in my faith. I believe that I'm called to be on this earth to help people and bring people to Christ. I can be a positive impact and a light in the world. This drives me daily. I can prove that anyone, with any past and from any circumstance, can overcome adversity and make a dent in this world. My goal is to inspire, motivate, and push people to become more.

That's my drive and that's why I can't lose. I refuse to give up on my life's purpose and this business is the vehicle to help me achieve it.

As huge as my goal is, it starts with One. One day—One conversation. Just like the process of creating wealth, I need to start with my daily focus on impacting the people around me. The more positive influence I spread, the more I can scale.

It's not some grandiose pipedream that consumes my day. It's the daily positive interactions and experiences that will eventually produce the compounding effect.

My wife and I reached a net worth of one million dollars by steadily doing the work. Purpose works the same way. Just focus on making daily, consistent impact and by the end of your life, you'll accomplish huge things. Life will keep giving you opportunities to show up and make an impact. You need to decide daily that you're in it to win it.

Just last week, I met with my mastermind group and we held a fundraiser for The Caring House Project. This organization builds homes in Haiti. We had a goal to raise $100,000. Our guys really rallied around this event and within 45 minutes, we raised $151,000!

It was amazing. It was the proudest moment I've ever had as a business owner. We'll be able to build an entire village with that money. This is what impact is about.

I'm hoping to launch more initiatives like this and continue developing housing for people around the world. Having a strong purpose has pushed me to this level and it can do the same for you.

You only have two choices in life: 1) To push yourself to reach your potential and 2) To ignore your potential. This is the choice that we all make, whether we realize it or not.

My friends, choose Option 1. Choose to live a life worth living. A life of abundance, impact, and purpose. If you and I commit to each other to live such a life, we can truly change the world and leave a legacy.

CHAPTER 8
LEGACY

On the topic of courage...

My father knew that if he left two children behind and arrived at the refugee camp in Austria, eventually the Red Cross would step in and try to reunite the children with them. He made a calculated decision and made his move.

It would be more than six months until I would see my brother, Dan, and my sister, Simona, again. My father chose to take me because I could walk, and he and my mother carried my two youngest siblings. You see, they used my ability to walk as a resource. They understood that I could walk on my own and my two younger siblings could be carried.

Fortunately, our story had a happy ending, unlike most stories that start out like mine. We were all able to escape communism. During the next year, the communist dictator in Romania was killed and our family was reunited at last. A year later, we were sponsored to come to Canada and start a new life. Growing up as the oldest of nine children, and having the responsibilities associated with being the oldest, I never forgot those vague memories of playing in the refugee camp, and never forgot the sacrifice and bravery of my two parents.

On the topic of money... Once you develop a mindset of "how", you will find that asking that question will force you to expand your reality. If you only have a vision of a small reality, you will always make small profits.

A final note here: Money always needs a home.

There's a ton of money available in North America, but very few good operators and stewards of money. In good times and in bad, that money will need to go somewhere. With bank savings rates at near zero, people are eager to find better returns. If the market crashes tomorrow, I know that I'll be getting phone calls looking for places to park money.

This is why someone like Warren Buffet has been so successful. He became a responsible steward and people trust him regardless of what the market does.

Become a great operator, and you'll never have a problem raising money.

I'll leave you with this thought...

Regardless of how you entered this life, you can alter how you exit. You have so much potential inside of you and if my message can be summed up to one point it's this:

Dream big, take massive action and have faith that you can accomplish extraordinary things.

BENIAMIN MURESAN

A CLOSING MESSAGE FROM MY PARENTS

[Dad] If you start something, that's the last day you're going to get stuck, my dear. Look around and take the first opportunity and just start.
There has to be an open door somewhere.
It's like a job. You have a dream job in mind, but it's not there yet.
Take the job you can get until you get to your dream job.
[Mom] Some people stand in front of a door and wait for somebody else to open it. But if you don't open the door yourself, it's not going to be opened. You have to open it.
Find a door and open it.
[Dad] And it's there. Start today. It's never too late.

I know that my parents are proud that I've opened so many doors for myself and have found success on the other side. The winding path I took to build my wealth doesn't compare with the harrowing journey that I took alongside my mother and father when I was a child. But, the story of how I moved from communism to capitalism is one I've been happy to share with you.

APPENDIX

Ben Muresan's Family Tree

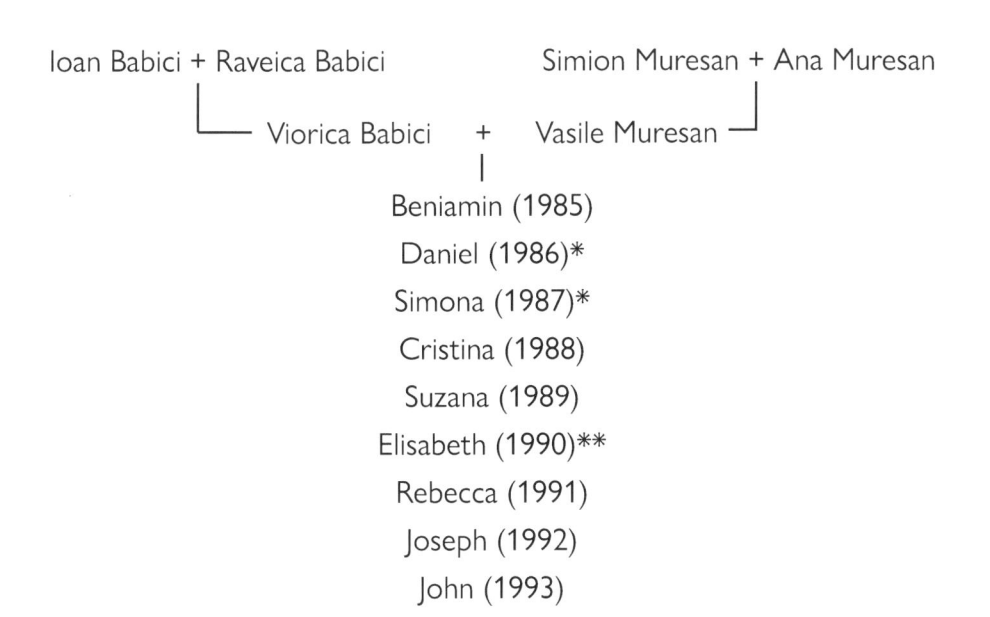

Ioan Babici + Raveica Babici   Simion Muresan + Ana Muresan
            └── Viorica Babici   +   Vasile Muresan ──┘
                            |
                    Beniamin (1985)
                    Daniel (1986)*
                    Simona (1987)*
                    Cristina (1988)
                    Suzana (1989)
                    Elisabeth (1990)**
                    Rebecca (1991)
                    Joseph (1992)
                    John (1993)

Note: Ben has a very large, extended family. However, for the purposes of this illustration, only his immediate family is listed.

* Left in Romania

** Born in Austria

APPENDIX

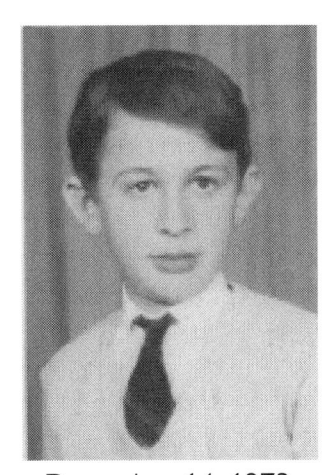

December 14, 1973.
Vasile. 12 years old.

1977. Vasile's baptism.

Circa 1980. Grandpa Simion Muresan.

BENIAMIN MURESAN

1981. Vasile in the army.

1981. Vasile in the army. He's the one kneeling and holding the corn.

APPENDIX

1981. Vasile in the army. He's the one in the middle with the guy on his shoulders.

1981. Vasile in the army. The one on the left.

1981. Vasile Muresan in the army.

APPENDIX

1982. Viorica splashing in the water.

1982. Aunt Maria and Viorica.

BENIAMIN MURESAN

1982. Viorica.

1983. Viorica, Vasile, and Aunt Maria.

APPENDIX

1983. Vasile and
Grandpa Ioan Babici.

1983. Vasile.

BENIAMIN MURESAN

Apr 10, 1984. Vasile and Viorica coming together in a civil union. Vasile and Viorica on the right, family members in the back. From left to right: Aunt Maria, Lidiuca (friend), and Grandma Ana Muresan

April 29, 1984. Vasile and Viorica at their wedding.

APPENDIX

April 29, 1984. Vasile and Viorica at their wedding.

April 29, 1984. Vasile and Viorica
at their wedding.

BENIAMIN MURESAN

1984. Viorica.

1986. Aunt Rodica, Ben, Vasile, and Viorica.

1986. Viorica, front right, and Vasile on accordion, middle back, among friends.

APPENDIX

1988. Vasile and Viorica with their kids. From left to right, Cristina, Dan, Ben, and Simona.

BENIAMIN MURESAN

1989. From left to right, front row: Simona and Suzana, back row: Ben, Cristina, and Dan.

APPENDIX

1989. Cristina and Simona.

1990. Ben and his siblings eating dinner in Austria

BENIAMIN MURESAN

January 15, 1990. Austrian refugee camp. Vasile holding Suzana on the left, Viorica holding Cristina in the middle right, and their friend holding Ben on the right.

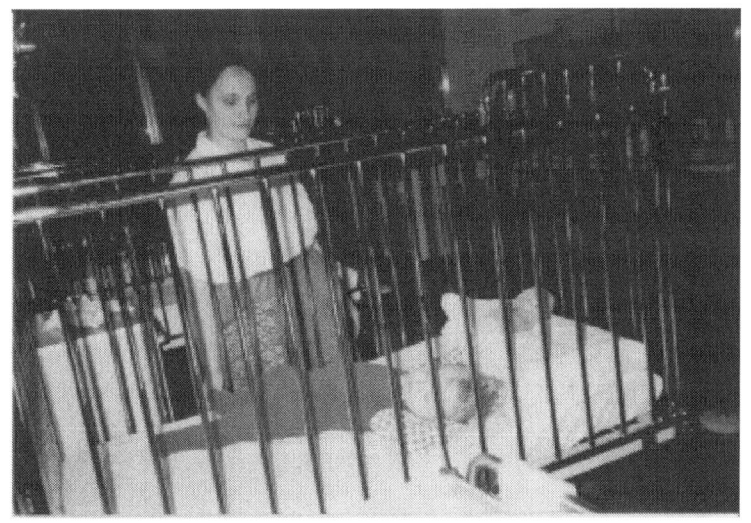

1990. Viorica watching Elisabeth (daughter she was pregnant with when she fled) sleeping in Austria.

APPENDIX

1991. Ben. Grade 1.

1991. Elisabeth, Simona, Rebecca, and Cristina.

BENIAMIN MURESAN

1991. Siblings. From left to right: Suzana, Daniel, Vinicius (cousin Vini), Rebecca, Cristina, and Ben.

1991. Simona, Ben, and Daniel.

APPENDIX

1991. Vasile feeding Rebecca. On the floor:
Suzana, Elisabeth, and Cristina.

1991. Vasile, kids, and Viorica.

BENIAMIN MURESAN

1991. Vasile, second from the left, and Viorica with the pink head scarf in the back; arriving in Toronto, Canada from Austria.

1993. Grandpa Ioan Babici and Grandma Raveica Babici holding Joseph.

APPENDIX

May 11, 1993. Grandpa Ioan Babici.

1993. Ben. Grade 3.

1994. Elisabeth, Joseph, John, Rebecca, Dan, and the Lumina van.

BENIAMIN MURESAN

2008. Grandma Ana
Muresan's 80th birthday.

APPENDIX

Newspaper article in Austria. Romanian family
with six children are waiting to immigrate to Canada.

BENIAMIN MURESAN

Newspaper article from when the Muresans
got their Canadian citizenship.

131

APPENDIX

Watch the full video of my parents telling their story at www.humble.ceo/c2c

RECOMMENDED READING AND RESOURCES

Brunson, Russell. (2020). Expert secrets, New York, NY: Hay House.

Cardone, Grant. (2011). The 10X Rule. Hoboken, NJ: John Wiley & Sons, Inc.

Conwell, Russell. (2018). Acres of Diamonds. Independently Published.

Evans, Mark, DM. (2018). The 10-Minute Business Owner. USA: DM Publishing.

Gerber, Michael. (2004). The E-myth Revisited. New York, NY: HarperCollins Publishers, Inc.

Kiyosaki, Robert. (2017). Rich Dad, Poor Dad. New York, NY: Warner Books, Inc.

Rood, Chris. (2018). The Source of the Deal. USA: Chris Rood, Publisher.

Schroeder, Alice. (2009). The Snowball: Warren Buffett and the Business of Life. New York, NY: Bantam Books.

Stanley, Thomas J. and Danko, William D. (2010). The Millionaire Next Door. Lanham, MD: Taylor Trade Publishing.

Brunson, Russell. YouTube Video: ClickFunnels: https://www.youtube.com/watch?v=7kkSC7jdnf8

Manufactured by Amazon.ca
Bolton, ON